Paul M. King

Effective School Leadership:

Developing Principals

Through Cognitive Coaching

Effective School Leadership: Developing Principals Through Cognitive Coaching

Jane Ellison and Carolee Hayes

Credits

Christopher-Gordon Publishers, Inc.
Bridging Theory and Practice

1502 Providence Highway, Suite 12
Norwood, MA 02062
800-934-8322 • 781-762-5577
www.Christopher-Gordon.com

Printed in Canada

10 9 8 7 6 5 4 3 2 1   09 08 07 06

ISBN: 1-929024-98-3

Library of Congress Catalogue Number: 2006921771

This book is dedicated to all the committed principals of public schools who work tirelessly to support staff and student learning and well-being, and to the Cognitive Coaching community that supports their work.

Contents

Foreword

To become a teacher, one must think like a teacher. To become a principal, one must think like a principal. It is not just what principals do that makes them exceptional, it is the knowledge, perceptions, cognition, and decisions that inform what they do. These skills can be developed in a coaching relationship. In a similar manner, to become an effective coach, one must learn to think like a coach. Just as we want teachers to develop reflective capacities, so, too, do we want to develop a principal's ability to think, plan, problem-resolve, and reflect in ways that are most consistently effective. Coaching a principal or a future principal to think like one, however, takes special skills and knowledge. That is what this book is about.

Effective School Leadership: Developing Principals Through Cognitive Coaching is a valuable resource for those who mentor, coach, or peer-mediate new and experienced principals. The authors are exceptionally well qualified on this topic. They draw from years of personal experiences in leadership positions as principals and staff developers. Each has coached innumerable principals—new ones, veterans, those struggling, and those seeking to improve already fine performance. They have designed, co-developed, and taught Cognitive Coaching seminars to thousands of educators in North and Central America. They develop and certify qualified Cognitive Coaches for school districts and educational agencies. In this book, they have done a remarkable job of synthesizing the essence of current research on leadership, the effects of coaching, adult development, trust building, and change. All of this is integrated into an easily readable flow of information that engages and sustains the reader.

Coaching models are proliferating. Many default to giving advice and telling. Well intentioned and helpful to principals, they often fail to achieve the profession-long change and self-directedness aimed for in Cognitive Coaching. Consulting—telling, advising, showing, and doing—is a more comfortable habit than mediating thinking and, being so, easy to revert to when one encounters coaching difficulties. Readers will find here the skills base necessary for successful coaching. Also here is a clear description of how the Cognitive Coach works to mediate another's perceptions, knowledge base, and decisions. No one approach, of course, fits all occasions, and readers will find information for when and how to incorporate consulting and collaborating in their work. For an understanding of the uniqueness of Cognitive Coaching in relation to other models, this book should be required reading.

This is a practical book that leaders most probably will keep close at hand—dog-eared and frequently referenced. It is grounded in research on the effects of Cognitive Coaching, the complexities of today's schools, the demands on principals and their staffs, and an unwavering commitment to excellence. One of the particular values of this book is the organization of practical examples of coaching conversations with principals. The reader will sense the authenticity of the conversations and can be guided by their structure and content through the examples. Of particular value are the notations of the coach's thinking and decisions as he or she engages the principals' reflection. Maps are provided for guiding planning, reflecting, and problem-resolving conversations.

The book's premise supports the novice coach in thinking like an expert coach. Novices in any field look at surface behaviors and actions. They might offer ideas about how to improve behaviors or make better choices. Experts, however, look beneath the surface and learn to intervene at the level of such cognitive skills as analysis, causal thinking, and visioning. Novice coaches, whose corrections focus primarily on behaviors, too often contribute to learning that is episodic: *I got it today, but I didn't generalize it for future use.* In reality, decisions are driven by the influence of prior experiences, craft knowledge, beliefs, values, mental models, and a sense of personal identity. Beneath these are less tangible resources, yet the most powerful of all in determining behavior. They are the wellspring of effectiveness: consciousness, efficacy, flexibility, craftsmanship, and interdependence. Illuminating this vast source of human potential is done through language. This book reveals ways to use language to coach at these levels for sustained, self-determined, and self-directed growth.

Arthur L. Costa
Granite Bay, CA

Robert J. Garmston,
El Dorado Hills, CA

Acknowledgments

This book could not have been written without the encouragement and support of our friends, families, and colleagues. Several years ago, Bruce Wellman acknowledged the work we were doing with principals and suggested that we should share our knowledge and expertise by writing a book. As we talked with others about the idea, principals, their supervisors, teachers, and staff developers echoed that sentiment. It became increasingly apparent that little support was being offered to principals in most districts and that such a book could make a difference to the culture of schools. Each time we mentioned the idea of a book about supporting principals with Cognitive Coaching, people validated the need and encouraged us to write it. When Hiram Howard and Sue Canavan of Christopher-Gordon Publishers expressed interest in the "hot topic" of coaching principals, we were compelled to begin the project.

Since little research has been conducted on the topic of coaching principals, we relied heavily on our 15 years of experience with it. We are indebted to the principals with whom we worked for teaching us about the kind of support they need and helping us to understand the stresses of their job. Several colleagues in the Cognitive Coaching community also embarked on coaching principals in their districts; their willingness to share their learning assisted us in developing the concepts and processes described in this book.

Of course, this work, or any other on Cognitive Coaching, would never have been possible without Bob Garmston and Art Costa, the co-developers of Cognitive Coaching. They continue to serve as role models of life-long learning to us all. Their spirits live in this work and in the Cognitive Coaching community at large.

Finally, we are grateful to our families for their continued support of our work and professional goals with their patience, understanding, and love.

Introduction

More than 20 years ago, Art Costa and Bob Garmston developed a process called Cognitive Coaching to support teachers in a manner very different from the traditional practices in public education. Their intention was to move beyond a behaviorist philosophy that often focused on instilling behaviors in a teacher's daily practice. In this practice, monitoring and evaluation were based on compliance with desired behaviors. Checklists were common as principals, with clipboard in hand, checked off teacher behaviors. Teachers' words and actions were commonly scripted, followed by a conversation in which the principal praised the correct behaviors and talked to the teacher about the missing behaviors.

Cognitive Coaching was a breath of fresh air to professional practice. It is grounded in the belief that the thought processes of the teacher drive the practice. Instead of seeking compliance, Cognitive Coaching develops thoughtful professionals who are self-directed. The Cognitive Coaching process is not rote or directive, but instead uses structures for supporting the teacher's own planning, reflecting, and problem-resolving. It is a set of tools designed specifically to enhance performance by supporting the teacher's internal thought processes.

The 20 years of research on coaching teachers with this methodology has shown the following significant results (Edwards, 2005):

- Cognitive Coaching is linked with increased student test scores and other benefits for students.

- Teachers grow in teaching efficacy.

- Cognitive Coaching impacts teacher thinking, causing them to be more reflective and to think in more complex ways.

- Teachers are more satisfied with their positions and with their choice of teaching as a profession.

- School cultures become more professional.

- Teachers collaborate more.

- Cognitive Coaching assists teachers professionally.

- Cognitive Coaching benefits teachers personally.

As Cognitive Coaching is more widely used in educational institutions, it has become clear that the skills and methods have an application beyond teacher supervision. Teachers realize that the process works well with students and enhances their thought processes. Principals find that Cognitive Coaching can be used in meetings to assist groups in working at higher levels and in being reflective in their practice. The skills of Cognitive Coaching also are useful with parents in conferring about their child's progress. Cognitive Coaching is a process that assists any group or individual in becoming more self-managing, self-monitoring, and self-modifying. These applications are described in our previous book, *Cognitive Coaching: Weaving the Threads of Learning and Change Into the Culture of an Organization.*

As practicing educators working with principals across the nation and internationally, we have been dismayed by the lack of authentic support for principals. Although institutes, conferences, and workshops are held on a frequent basis, there is little or nothing that reflects job-embedded professional development. Principals are typically given the keys to the building, a pat on the back, and wishes of good luck. They are probably the least supervised of all school professionals and yet are among the most vulnerable. Their work is a critical factor in student learning. We believe that the current situation constitutes a crisis in leadership in public education. Without a well-developed support system for principals, more will struggle and some will fail. More students will be affected. Robert Marzano's research on school and teacher impact on student achievement informs us that up to 20% of the variation in student achievement is based on school-related factors (Miller, 2003). Who can better address those school factors than strong principals? Who will want to become a principal? Professionals will question whether the demands of the job are worth the sacrifices.

We write this book as a manifesto—calling for a rethinking of the structures and processes to ensure the success and leadership of principals. That success, we believe, drives the success of teachers and students. Principals are being asked to do more and more with less and less. Our experience indicates that when principals are supported by coaching, it impacts their efficacy, consciousness, interdependence, flexibility, and craftsmanship. They are also able to internalize the processes for supporting teachers, students, and parents in those same five domains. If school systems are truly committed to raising the achievement of all students, they must make the same commitment to principals. All principals inherently deserve an ongoing system of support, tailored to their unique needs and those of their schools. Although we realize that coaching principals is not a cure-all or even a simple process, we are certain that it will make a difference to all stakeholders in schools. We draw from the Capistrano Unified School District in California, using the wisdom of the Chinese: "If you want one year of prosperity, grow grain. If you want 10 years of prosperity, grow trees. If you want 100 years of prosperity, grow people" (Lovely, 1999).

We believe that if a rigorous system is developed for the Cognitive Coaching of principals, many of the same gains that have been achieved for teachers will be achieved with principals. We advocate Cognitive Coaching for all principals, not just those new to the profession.

This book develops a vision of coaching through the consideration of six major themes:

Chapter 1, "The Evolving Principalship: The Challenges Ahead," explores the changing nature of the principalship, focusing on the current state of the principalship, new visions emerging for the future, and how we can support principals in moving toward those new visions.

Chapter 2, "Cognitive Coaching for Principals," describes the intentions, purposes, and processes of Cognitive Coaching. It serves as a review for those familiar with Cognitive Coaching, and is an introduction to the model for supporting principals for those who do not have a background in coaching.

Chapter 3, "The Effect of Supporting Principals With Cognitive Coaching," offers a view of how a principal's life might change if Cognitive Coaching were a routine part of the support system. One action research project is described in detail as a means of depicting the possibilities of coaching principals.

Chapter 4, "Who Should Provide Cognitive Coaching to Principals?", provides guidance to districts that want to incorporate Cognitive Coaching into the support system for principals. Decision points and questions to consider are outlined for reflection and action.

Chapter 5, "The Thinking of a Principal's Cognitive Coach," gives the reader insight into the metacognition of a Cognitive Coach. Understanding how a coach thinks is the key to developing the skills and capabilities of coaching.

Chapter 6, "Options and Structures for Providing Cognitive Coaching to Principals," explores the various ways a system might implement a coaching program for principals. It offers key implementation questions for consideration and a variety of delivery models.

We invite you to explore the ideas of this book and consider how they might make a difference in your school. Theodore Roosevelt once said, "This country will not be a good place for any of us to live in unless we make it a good place for all of us to live in." We believe that is true for all members of the school community. Cognitive Coaching has been recognized as a means by which to support students, parents, and teachers. It must become an institutionalized process for principals as well.

References

Edwards, J. (2005). *Cognitive Coaching: A synthesis of the research.* Highlands Ranch, CO: Center for Cognitive Coaching.

Lovely, S. (1999, September). Developing leaders from within. *Educational Leadership,* 29 (1).

Miller, K. (2003, November). "School, teacher, and leadership impacts on student achievement." *McREL Policy Brief,* p. 1.

1

The Evolving Principalship: The Challenges Ahead

Imagine yourself as the superintendent of a school district. You are very familiar with the large body of research pointing to the principal as the key player in the success of a school for both its teachers and its students. Your current principals seem highly stressed, and some are even burned out. As you search for the best and the brightest to fill principal positions, you find fewer and fewer leaders attracted to the job. In fact, in the last 5 years you have seen talented people choosing to leave as well as new principals failing at their jobs. How can you increase the attractiveness of the job and make sure that those coming into the job will be successful? If great principals, like great teachers, are developed and not born, then as a wise superintendent you will be thoughtful and strategic in providing processes by which to enhance the growth and development of all principals.

The face of the principalship is changing; so too are the faces occupying the principal's office. One reason is the massive retirement of baby boomers. U.S. Labor Department studies show that more than 40% of school principals will soon retire, and 42% of school districts also report a shortage of highly qualified candidates for principal openings (Savoye, 2001). The successful future of public schools demands that we develop a new generation of leaders and help our current leaders face the changing horizons before us. Public education has put significant effort and resources into providing induction programs for new teachers and ongoing professional development for veteran teachers. The same cannot be said for principals. Our nation has legislated the expectation of a highly qualified teacher in every classroom, but has the same commitment been made to having a highly qualified principal in every school? The answer is clearly no.

To address the leadership challenges for tomorrow's schools, careful consideration must be given to the current picture of principals' work. Two compelling questions logically follow that conclusion:

- How must the view of the principalship be re-created to adapt to a changing educational scene?

- As the vision of the principalship changes, how will systems respond in order to create the human resource capacity that is required?

This chapter addresses these critical issues.

The Face of Today's Principalship

One of the authors' recent coaching sessions with a veteran principal characterizes the challenges facing many principals today. This 12-year veteran principal, reflecting on her new position, related that she had previously worked in a school that was struggling with student achievement. The school worked hard and raised students' achievement to a 75% proficiency rate, yet that was not enough. Her new school is at 98% proficiency, yet that is not enough. She feels challenged to become a different kind of principal. Internally she is troubled by the fact that no matter what she accomplishes as a leader, it is not enough. This principal is seeking a new vision for how she might work, and she doesn't know where to go for the future.

This principal describes the principalship as changing from a managerial position to a role that is first and foremost attentive to student learning. For the first time in history, under the No Child Left Behind Act of 2001, principals whose schools do not make adequate yearly progress (AYP) may be removed. A district-level leader in Colorado expressed the current state for principals under this act:

> The stress of Accreditation and Adequate Yearly Progress magnifies the stress on principals as they worry about their school making it. As targets increase and sanctions are more frightening, principals feel the incredible stress. The principal must be an instructional leader and be able to manage many change efforts effectively. They must be able to bring about significant instructional improvement in a short amount of time, defying the research on implementing change.

Statistics from the Department of Labor indicate that many potential principal candidates are turning away from the job because compensation is insufficient compared to the responsibilities, too much time is required, and the job is too stressful (NAESP, 2002).

One principal wrote these words about her job today:

> Principals now supervise before- and after-school childcare programs, extended-day kindergarten or childcare for kindies during the day. They also are responsible for monitoring numerous school and district assessments and a multitude of programs that didn't exist several years ago. Several have been added, and few have been discontinued. Specialized reading programs and English acquisition programs have built-in accountability pieces, which are all important and they demand time, focus, and follow-through. Technology alone often involves

developing implementation plans and monitoring from year to year in order to attempt to stay current. At the moment, every principal…feels the press of CBLA [Colorado Basic Literacy Act] requirements, No Child Left Behind expectations, and IDEA [Individuals With Disabilities Education Act] redesign initiatives. It is a challenge to remain thoughtful and deliberate when making decisions about staff development or any "next steps" that are necessary in school improvement efforts.

There is no question that the job of the principal is more demanding and stress producing than in the past. In an informal survey of school administrators in 13 states and Canada, the following questions were asked:

What kind of support does your district provide for principals?

What district-provided professional development is offered for principals?

What observations would you make about the stress level of principals?

What observations might you make about principals being Cognitively Coached?

All 30 respondents indicated that principals were highly stressed. One principal in the survey reported, "My blood pressure lowered 25 points after retirement. Personal safety and security for all provided the most stress for me. The pressure of the political environment surrounding schools was an additional contributor."

> *"My blood pressure lowered 25 points after retirement. Personal safety and security for all provided the most stress for me. The pressure of the political environment surrounding schools was an additional contributor."*

The number one source of stress reported by more than a third of respondents was the AYP expectations under No Child Left Behind. Other sources of stress varied and included the following:

- The loneliness of the elementary principalship
- The long hours of the high school principalship
- The demanding nature of today's at-risk students
- The level of change that is being implemented
- Being pulled out of one's building for district meetings
- Safety and security concerns
- Being admonished rather than supported
- The teacher association
- Guilt about not being instructional leaders
- Continual reassignments at the last minute
- The "boiled frog" syndrome. A frog that is put in hot water will jump out, but if it is put in cool water whose temperature is gradually raised over time, it will boil to death, not knowing that it is getting hotter. Principals feel things are slowly becoming more stressful and that they are boiling slowly in the juices of stress.

Only one respondent reported that the stress level seemed manageable. Another respondent spoke poignantly about her work: "The kids and the staff keep me going. I don't love the principalship. I like being a principal at my building. If they moved me, I'd have to question whether I would continue in this job."

A study in Colorado reported that stress for first-time principals stemmed from three causes: absorbing volumes of information, working for change despite significant resistance, and proving oneself to others (Lovely, 2004). When you consider the cumulative effect of many stressors, the totality of it becomes daunting.

Besides the principalship losing its attraction due to the stresses of the job, few principals come into the job fully prepared. There is widespread agreement in the educational research community that programs that train principals are inadequate. In its 2003 study on educating school leaders led by Arthur Levine, the Center for Reinventing Public Education (Sanders, 2005) found that principal licensing programs provide little specialized coursework. The coursework that is provided is often a generic menu of education courses, such as educational psychology or research methods, unrelated to the daily work of principals and certainly not focused on leading learning communities. The study also found that only 6% of university faculty had ever served in the capacity of the principal. Of those who had participated in coursework for principal licensing, 90% believed that the preparation they received did not adequately prepare them to cope with the demands of the principalship. Dealing with in-school politics, working with parents and other constituents, and handling test-based accountability were the topics that principals felt least prepared to handle (Archer, 2005).

Even when licensing is achieved, a recent study showed that fewer than half of licensed principals are willing to consider the job (Cusick, 2003). Many educators complete licensing requirements as part of a masters program merely to qualify for a pay raise.

For those who have licenses and are experienced, there is little expectation that new skills be developed. According to our informal survey results, principal professional development is random and lacking in focus on student learning outcomes. An educator who recently renewed her principal's license reported that all that was required was documentation of 90 hours of professional growth. Included were conference attendance, presentations, in-service hours, and coursework. Documentation of learning outcomes was absent; paperwork required documentation only of seat time. It is clear that today's principals are not required to develop new skills that fit the changing demands of the principalship by relicensing requirements.

How Principals Are Being Supported

When the 30 survey participants were asked how principals were supported, only 11 indicated that formal mentoring programs were in place, and those were only for first-year principals. Seven said there was informal mentoring. A common means of support, mentioned by half of the respondents, was quarterly or monthly principal meetings. Six respondents mentioned the importance of phone access to central office staff. Only one said that frequent visits to the school were part of the support offered. Two said that coaches for teachers were important sources of support. Many of the respondents noted that stress symptoms seemed to be coming earlier each year. Others reported burnout and thoughts of retirement.

The 30 survey participants were asked how the district provided professional development to principals, with a list of offerings that included 23 topics. Ten said that the district held institutes and academies for principals. Five mentioned that they were able to attend national conferences. Topics for professional development showed wide variation, from Cognitive Coaching training to child-abuse and cooperative-learning training. Six indicated that professional development for principals was situational, usually a reaction to some need such as fair hiring practices or diversity training. Four participants mentioned informal support groups established among principals to meet their own needs. Only 10 of the 23 topics mentioned were specifically tied to best practices for instruction and student learning. The others were related to the teacher evaluation, child abuse, technology, and so forth.

The survey participants expressed value for the process of coaching, but they clearly indicated that their systems did not consider coaching of principals to be a high priority or an institutionalized value. The deterrents included time for coaching, understanding of the value of the process, and skill levels of those supporting principals. When district leaders reflect on the support they give to principals, many conclude that they are not doing enough. A news reporter for the *Baltimore Sun Times* (Loh, 2005) quotes Frank DeStefano, a district-level leader, speaking about a new principal in his district: "She's having a difficult year and it's much less reflective of her and much more reflective of our not supporting the school correctly."

The Future Face of the Principalship

Having considered the existing state of the principalship, we turn now to a compelling question: How should the view of the principalship be re-created to adapt to a changing educational scene? First we consider the context of the job of principal. How is the principal's environment today different from that of the past decades? Table 1-1 (Wellman & Lipton, 2004) describes four driving forces of school change.

Table 1-1. Four Driving Forces of School Change

Shifting From	Shifting To
A teaching focus	A learning focus
Teaching as private practice	Teaching as collaborative practice
School improvement as an option	School improvement as a requirement
Accountability	Responsibility

Shifting From a Teaching Focus to a Learning Focus

Historically, principals have been charged with supervising and evaluating the performance of the teacher
based on a prescribed set of teaching criteria and standards. Most teacher evaluation systems contain little or no
mention of student learning. The focus of principals' work
has been on judging and supporting teachers' instruction
instead of judging and supporting student learning. Teachers could have low-performing students and continue to
receive positive evaluations. Many evaluations focused on
classroom management, attendance at professional development seminars, service to the staff, and other managerial issues such as planning.

Today's world of standards-based education has shifted the focus from the teacher's activities to the results of
children's learning. It is no longer acceptable to have students who are not learning. The expression "I taught it;
they just didn't learn it" is inexcusable.

What this means for principals is that they will have
to work differently with teachers. They will be required
to coach teachers from a focus on student learning instead
of on teacher actions. That means they will have to understand the goals of instruction and consider how teaching
is only a means to the end of learning. The shift from a
focus on teaching to a focus on learning requires a movement away from keeping teachers happy and productive
to a conscious monitoring of data related to student learning and engaging teachers in ongoing dialogue and discussion about student learning.

Shifting From Teaching as Private Practice to Teaching as Collaborative Practice

The culture of schools has traditionally been one of
solitude and autonomy. Teachers have been the kings and
queens of their classrooms, making decisions that were
unquestioned. It was not unusual in the past for a teacher

to work as a solo practitioner. Every day a teacher determined what would be taught, how it would be taught, and how it would be assessed. Results varied from classroom to classroom and that was acceptable.

With standards-based education, however, there is a need to think differently. Teachers must collaborate on the meaning of standards and on how they will be assessed. Without such collaboration, there are no standards, only random approximations of the standards. Thus the daily world of the teacher has shifted from one of isolation and autonomy to one that is based on ongoing collaboration regarding student learning.

The impact of such a shift for principals is dramatic. The principal has to move beyond managing individuals to creating cultures of collaboration. The principal is truly the lead learner and facilitator of meaningful dialogue. The principal's job is to create teacher networks that serve learners and ensure an ongoing study of student learning. The skill set of the principal is dramatically different. It requires a focus on systems thinking and an understanding of the processes of group development. The work of a principal goes far beyond instructional leader; it encompasses instructional leadership under the larger umbrella of organization developer. With the focus on being an organization developer, the principal promotes instructional leadership across the entire school staff.

Shifting From School Improvement as an Option to School Improvement as a Requirement.

School improvement has long been a cliché in educational circles with little substantive meaning. School improvement plans have often focused on school climate, curricular change, or professional development with little emphasis on what was actually happening with student learning. The standards movement has now focused educators' thinking on student learning. In many districts in the past, it was well known by parents and educators which schools were successful and which were not. Little attention was directed at changing those schools that were not as successful.

Today, given new legislative guidelines and changing expectations, school improvement is being specifically defined as AYP. Measurements are explicit, and expectations have been raised. Schools in which improvement is not achieved are being taken over by other entities. The principal's job is no longer about management but is clearly about driving change and improved achievement for students. The principal of the future must be data driven, a leader of change, and focused on student learning. The job will be about creating professional communities that define themselves through collecting, analyzing, and responding to data.

Shifting From Accountability to Responsibility

Accountability has been the hallmark of the last decade in education. Individual school results are reported in the press. As data management systems become more and more sophisticated, it is now possible to examine results for individual teachers. Schools are being sanctioned through a variety of legislative processes, including a takeover by state governments and charters. There is no longer a way to hide poor results. External evaluation is a norm.

The principal of the future will have to move beyond the accountability mentality, which focuses on external drivers, to a mentality that looks internally. How does a principal develop a staff that examines its own results on a regular basis? What kind of leadership moves a school from a mentality of oppression by external entities to a mentality that examines its learner goals and its achievement in relation to those goals? Clearly, a principal who leads for shared responsibility must work differently from a traditional principal. The challenge ahead requires us to think differently about how to develop principals for this changing face of the principalship.

If the No Child Left Behind Act of 2001 had included guidelines for highly qualified principals, what would they be? The answers are coming from many sources. The Interstate School Leaders License Consortium (ISLLC) produced the ISLLC Standards for School Leaders in 1996 (Hessel & Holloway, 2002), shown in Table 1-2.

Table 1-2. ISLLC Standards for School Leaders

Standard 1. A school administrator is an educational leader who promotes the success of all students by facilitating the development, articulation, implementation, and stewardship of a vision of learning that is shared and supported by the school community.

Standard 2. A school administrator is an educational leader who promotes the success of all students by advocating, nurturing, and sustaining a school culture and instructional program conducive to student learning and staff professional growth.

Standard 3. A school administrator is an educational leader who promotes the success of all students by ensuring management of the organization, operations, and resources for a safe, efficient, and effective learning environment.

Standard 4. A school administrator is an educational leader who promotes the success of all students by collaborating with families and community members, responding to diverse community interests and needs, and mobilizing community resources.

Standard 5. A school administrator is an educational leader who promotes the success of all students by acting with integrity, with fairness, and in an ethical manner.

Standard 6. A school administrator is an educational leader who promotes the success of all students by understanding, responding to, and influencing the larger political, social, economic, legal, and cultural contexts.

In addition to the six standards defined by ISLLC, there are approximately 200 indicators that delineate the meaning of the standards. The indicators are categorized by knowledge, disposition, and performance. Rubrics have been developed with four levels of performance—rudimentary, developing, proficient, and accomplished—for each of the standards. Many school districts are using these standards to realign their evaluation systems for principals. Universities and state governments are also using the ISLLC standards for licensing decisions. The ISLLC standards for principals clearly go far beyond management—making sure the books are ordered and the buses arrive on time.

The National Staff Development Council recently called for a change in the role of the principal:

> Now is the time to have a proper burial for the antiquated and dysfunctional role of principals. Let's put to rest the notion that school leadership is synonymous with charismatic, top-down, autocratic leadership. After we have paid our respects to the old way of school leadership, we must begin to embrace a vibrant new kind of leadership that is generated from inside out and bottom up. The real work of principals becomes that of supervising learning versus supervising teaching. The viability of future generations of teachers and students to thrive is largely dependent on principals making this shift. (Childs-Bowen, 2005)

The Center on Reinventing Public Education (Portin et al., 2003) interviewed 150 leaders in 21 schools and 4 states. The study delved into what principals actually do, unlike the ISLLC effort, which defined what principals *should* do. A key finding was the importance of diagnostic skills in principals. That is, no matter what the characteristics of the school (e.g., charter, elementary, middle, high, low or high socioeconomic), the principal must understand the needs of the school and be responsive to them. This sounds deceptively simple, but the ability to assess and respond is complex and challenging.

In addition, Portin reported that due to the unique challenges of each school, not every school needs the same leader. To define the job as instructional leadership might miss the point in some schools; the definition is too narrow and limiting. Instead, Portin suggested that there are many metaphorical ways to be a principal, depending on the diagnosed needs of the school: a one-man band, the leader of a jazz combo, or the conductor of an orchestra. The study found seven key areas of leadership that principals said a principal should attend to in leading a school (Table 1-3). The emphasis in each category will vary according to the diagnosis of the school's needs.

Table 1-3. Seven Key Leadership Areas

Instructional

Ensuring quality of instruction, modeling teaching practice, supervising curriculum, and Ensuring quality of teaching resources.

Cultural

Guiding the symbolic resources of the school, e.g., its traditions, climate, and history

---

Managerial

Overseeing the operations of the school, e.g., its budget, schedule, facilities, safety and security, and transportation.

Human Resource

Recruiting, hiring, firing, inducting, and mentoring teachers and administrators; developing leadership capacity and professional development opportunities

cont.

| **Strategic** |
| Promoting vision, mission, and goals—and developing a means by which to reach them |
| **External Development** |
| Representing the school in the community, developing capital, public relations, recruiting students, buffering and mediating external interests, and advocating for the school's interests |
| **Micropolitical** |
| Buffering and mediating internal interests, while maximizing resources (financial and human) |

Finally, Portin's study suggested that the capacity of a principal to lead will vary greatly depending on local conditions, such as budget constraints, labor relations, and human resource issues.

Another body of work is influencing expectations for today's and future principals. Mid-continent Research for Education and Learning (McREL) has conducted a meta-analysis of 30 years of research on what leadership qualities relate to student achievement (Marzano, Waters, & McNulty, 2005). This is particularly important research because for the first time an effort has been made to move beyond personal anecdotes, theories, and observations to take a hard look at more than 5,000 studies related to school leadership and student achievement. The study identified 21 leadership responsibilities that are significantly associated with student achievement (Table 1-4).

Marzano et al. (2005) are careful to stress that these leadership responsibilities are not a checklist to use for evaluation. They also point out that the emphasis should not be only on those with the highest correlations to student achievement. Instead, leadership has a situational nature, and some responsibilities will require greater

Table 1-4. Leadership Responsibilities and Student Achievement

Responsibility	The Extent to Which the Principal...	Correlation With Student Achievement
Affirmation	Recognizes and celebrates accomplishments and acknowledges failures	.19
Change Agent	Is willing to be challenged and actively challenges the status quo	.25
Contingent Rewards	Recognizes and rewards individual accomplishments	.24
Communi-cation	Establishes strong lines of communication with and among teachers and students	.23
Culture	Fosters shared beliefs and a sense of community and cooperation	.25
Discipline	Protects teachers from issues and influences that would detract from their teaching time or focus	.27
Flexibility	Adapts his or her leadership behavior to the needs of the current situation and is comfortable with dissent	.28
Focus	Establishes clear goals and keeps those goals in the forefront of the school's attention	.24

cont.

Ideals and Beliefs	Communicates and operates from strong ideals and beliefs about schooling	.22
Input	Involves teachers in the design and implementation of important decisions and policies	.25
Intellectual Stimulation	Ensures that faculty and staff are aware of the most current theories and practices and makes the discussion of these a regular aspect of the school's culture	.24
Involvement in Curriculum, Instruction, and Assessment	Is directly involved in the design and implementation of curriculum, instruction, and assessment	.20
Knowledge of Curriculum, Instruction, and Assessment	Is knowledgeable about current curriculum, instruction, and assessment practices	.25
Monitoring and Evaluating	Monitors the effectiveness of school practices and their impact on student learning	.27
Optimizer	Inspires and leads new and challenging innovations	.20
Order	Establishes a set of standard operating procedures and routines	.25

cont.

Outreach	Is an advocate and spokesperson for the school to all stakeholders	.27
Relationships	Demonstrates an awareness of the personal aspects of teacher and staff	.18
Resources	Provides teachers with materials and professional development necessary for the successful execution of their jobs	.25
Situational Awareness	Is aware of the details and undercurrents in the running of the school and uses information to address current and potential problems	.33
Visibility	Has quality contact and interactions with teachers and students	.20

emphasis depending on the circumstances in the school. The level of change occurring in the school is a critical factor to consider, because first-order change require different kinds of leadership than second-order change. First-order change usually occurs in small steps, whereas second-order change is a significant transformation in mental models and systemic structures. The key point of this research is that if a leader's capacity is developed in the appropriate responsibilities, student achievement will be positively impacted.

It is clear from various groups' attempts to define the qualities of future principals that there is not one recipe. It is also clear that what was once a simple managerial job has evolved into a complex leadership position requiring high levels of skill and knowledge. It is that very complexity that drives the case for providing Cognitive Coaching for principals.

Cognitive Coaching Support for the Development of Successful Principals

A key question that was introduced early in this chapter is: As the vision of the principalship changes, how will systems respond in order to create the human resource capacity that is required? To answer the question requires new thinking about how principals are developed. In Portin et al. (2003), most principals stated they had learned the skills of the principalship on the job and that little or nothing in their training had prepared them for the job. There is little evidence that education systems have deliberately put structures in place to develop the knowledge and skills of principals, yet there is significant research suggesting that the declarative and procedural knowledge of principals can be defined in such a manner that it can impact student achievement, the ultimate goal of a principal's work. Declarative knowledge is the information (e.g., facts, concepts, generalizations) that we know and understand; examples might be knowledge of personnel law or due process. Procedural knowledge consists of the skills and processes we apply to our declarative knowledge. When principals build a schedule, mediate conflict, counsel a parent, or build a budget, they are using procedural knowledge. As the studies we have cited indicated, both kinds of knowledge are necessary for today's principals.

Research on how people learn declarative and procedural knowledge (Marzano, 1992) informs us on how principals can develop both knowledge and skill in their jobs. The following steps for learning declarative knowledge are interrelated:

- Construct meaning and link new information to prior knowledge
- Organize and identify patterns in the information
- Store and embed the information in long-term memory

The following steps for learning procedural knowledge are more separate:

- Construct models and envision the steps of the process
- Shape the process to modify it and increase understanding of it
- Internalize the skill or process to achieve automaticity and fluency

As you will see in chapter 2, Cognitive Coaching is a process that is highly congruent with the processes required to learn both declarative and procedural knowledge. It is a means for: (a) reflecting on practice, (b) planning for future application, and (c) problem resolving. In using all three of these processes, the coach assists the principal in all of the steps required for learning both declarative and procedural knowledge. The State of Mind of consciousness is mediated by a coach in a manner that allows the principal to attend to the metacognitive processes of learning and decision making. Without mediation of thinking, over time, principals, like their students, are unlikely to internalize the knowledge and skills required to be successful in a multifaceted and demanding profession.

Cognitive Coaching supports and develops the thinking of the leader. If we know what kinds of thinking we need in leaders, how do we ensure that they are supported in becoming professionals who think like highly skilled principals? Ellen Condliffe Lagemann (2004), dean of Harvard's Graduate School of Education, provides an interesting interpretation of the differences in the use of the case method to develop different professionals at Harvard:

At the Harvard Law School, for example, cases are actual legal opinions. Students read them and professors teach them via the Socratic method, calling (without warning) on students and asking them questions that force them to reason to the essence of the legal precedent set by the case. At the Harvard Business School, members of the faculty write cases that describe "real world" problems in business, government, or the nonprofit sector, and students are asked to analyze those problems in study groups. Then, in class, professors ask volunteers to tell them what they would do to resolve the problem at hand. At the Harvard Medical School, meanwhile, cases are very short, often only a paragraph. The cases are given to students in class, where they immediately pool whatever they do and do not know about the situation with which they have been presented. They then agree on who will do research about specific, unresolved questions and, then, come together again to pool and refine their knowledge before once again going off to do further research.

Implicit in these different approaches to case teaching are different ways of thinking and acting. The law school is teaching students to reason from precedent—to think like a lawyer. The business school is teaching students to make decisions and take action—to act like a manager. And the medical school is teaching students to diagnose an illness–to reason like a doctor.

Cognitive Coaching is a way to develop leaders who think like principals. Without attention to the internal cognitive processes of principals, there is little likelihood that they will practice the thoughtful leadership that Harvard tries

Cognitive Coaching is a way to develop leaders who think like principals.

to develop in its lawyers, doctors, and businesspeople.

When principals are coached, we can expect changes in their cognitive processes. Some anecdotal reports are as follows:

> Those who are actually coached are not only able to solve the challenges in front of them, but are also able to apply their learning to new situations. Those who are supported in other ways, such as through consultation or advisement are greatly appreciative, but I am not sure they are developing the same level of capacity for solving future leadership challenges.

> [Principals who are coached have] greater consciousness of their decisions and the impact of the decisions made. [They are] more efficacious in their conversations about instruction (or any issue) with teachers. Also, I find that principals who are coached respond to problems that arise with greater ease. You can hear their resourcefulness in what they say. I also hear principals being able to see beyond the murkiness of a problem to the next steps or the end in mind-desired state. This brings their stress down, which impacts their relationships with teachers.

> The principals liked the support. They feel like they are being heard. It has been helpful to have someone else assist in solving problems; they are more willing to look at change. They feel revitalized. It gives them hope. It breaks the isolation. People feel more efficacious and it has raised their consciousness about standards.

> As I spend more time with folks and have more opportunities to coach, I am very aware that the level of trust is increasing and my principals are able to take more risks, not feel like they have to have "the right" answer and are more likely to simply share their thinking with me, not ask my permission to do whatever is on their mind.

There is certainly a need for more research on the effects on principals of being coached. We hope that some will be done in the next decade as school districts respond to the need to provide Cognitive Coaching to principals.

We have a sacred responsibility to the children of our country and our future leaders to dedicate ourselves to their development and improvement. If we do not, we are condoning leaders to work in isolation with limited resources for their professional growth. As we continue, we will build a vision of just how to do so in ways that are more effective than past practices.

References

Archer, J. (2005). Study blasts leadership preparation. *Education Week*, 24 (27), 1, 18.

Childs-Bowen, D. (2005). Rest in peace, charming all powerful principal. *Journal of Staff Development*, 26 (4), 7.

Cusick, P. A. (2003). The principalship? No thanks. *Education Week*, 22 (36), 3, 44, 34.

Hessel, K., & Holloway, J. (2002). *A framework for school leaders: Linking the ISLLC standards to practice*. Princeton, NJ: Educational Testing Services.

Lagemann, E. C. (2004). Toward a strong profession. *Education Week*, 23 (24), 48, 36–37.

Loh, L. (2005). Learning curve: New principals at city schools find varying levels of support. *Baltimore Sun Times*, July 17.

Lovely, S. (2004, June). Scaffolding for new leaders: Coaching and mentoring helps rookie principals grow on the job and gain confidence. *School Administrator*.

Marzano, R. (1992). *A different kind of classroom: Teaching with dimensions of learning*. Alexandria, VA: Association of Supervision and Curriculum Development.

Marzano, R., Waters, T., & McNulty, B. (2005). *School leadership that works*. Alexandria, VA: Association for Supervision and Curriculum Development.

National Association of Elementary School Principals (NAESP). (2002). *NAESP fact sheet on the principal shortage.* Unpublished pamphlet.

Portin, B., et al. (2003). *Making sense of leading schools: A study of the school principalship.* Seattle, WA: Center on Reinventing Public Education.

Sanders, T. (2005). Preparing school leaders shared responsibilities. *Education Week, 24* (30) 36–37.

Savoye, C. (2001). Fewer step forward to be school principals. *Christian Science Monitor,* October 2.

Wellman, B., & Lipton, L. (2004). *Data-driven dialogue.* Sherman, CT: MiraVia.

2

Cognitive Coaching for Principals

Humans don't get ideas; they make ideas.
—Art Costa and Robert Garmston

Cognitive Coaching supports individuals and workplace cultures that value reflection, complex thinking, and transformational learning. Leaders influence and develop the values, beliefs, assumptions, and ways of working in an organization. The context of leadership may vary, but the results of leadership have predictable patterns. An authoritarian leader creates a culture of fear and compliance. A laissez-faire leader creates a culture of chaos and uncertainty. A leader who intentionally uses Cognitive Coaching creates a culture of thoughtfulness and self-directed learning. What are the elements and constructs used by such a leader? This chapter provides a framework for the basic constructs of Cognitive Coaching of principals. Principals and principal supporters who choose to embrace this way of working will benefit from taking more extensive training in the principles and practices of Cognitive Coaching (Center for Cognitive Coaching, 2005).

The Mission of Cognitive Coaching

> *The mission of Cognitive Coaching is to produce self-directed persons with the cognitive capacity for high performance both independently and as members of a community.*

Developed in 1984 by Arthur Costa and Robert Garmston, Cognitive Coaching is a model that guides a leader's actions. "The mission of Cognitive Coaching is to produce self-directed persons with the cognitive capacity for high performance both independently and as members of a community" (Costa & Garmston, 2002, p. 16). Missions define an institution's purpose and reason for existing. Cognitive Coaching assists leaders in defining their purpose and role as leaders. Each word in the mission statement clarifies a way of working with intentionality.

The verb *produce* suggests that leaders must be results oriented, with a focus on outcomes for the individuals they lead. A leader who does not intentionally strive for clear expectations in the work of his or her followers is unlikely to have significant impact. Cognitive Coaching focuses on impact by assisting the leader in identifying the results that he or she is striving for and clarifying the success indicators and strategies for doing so. The cognitive coach also assists the leader in examining data, reflecting on its meaning, and committing to action for the future.

Self-directed persons are one of the outcomes of a leader who holds the mission of Cognitive Coaching in the forefront of his or her mind. Costa and Garmston define self-directedness through three distinct yet intertwined qualities: self-managing, self-monitoring, and self-modifying.

The self-managing person is able to articulate goals and intentions. He holds a clear vision for his own achievement and is strategic in planning for goal achievement. Self-management includes specificity about indicators of success. A person with skill in self-management is deliberate about considering prior knowledge and experiences. She is careful to control the tendency to leap to action, instead gathering information and considering options and relevant data.

Self-monitoring requires constant vigilance of oneself and one's environment. The self-monitoring person is gathering data as an ongoing process. He draws on self-knowledge as a checkpoint for attending to what is working and not working. Self-monitoring is a process requiring attention to one's metacognition as well as external cues. In self-monitoring, an individual is constantly comparing the current conditions to the intended plan. To be truly self-monitoring requires attention to alternatives and choice making in the moment. It demands focus through attentive listening and observing.

To be self-modifying, an individual must evaluate her actions and decisions in terms of her intentions and goals. Self-modification requires reflection and introspection. A disposition toward continuous growth serves the self-modifying leader. That disposition includes constructing meaning from experience and commitment to make changes based on the new learning. Self-modification draws from the self-monitoring process to focus forward and deliberate on future actions.

The phrase *cognitive capacity* differentiates Cognitive Coaching from other models of coaching or supervision. The unique focus of this work is to develop an individual's ability to engage in higher level cognitive functioning (e.g., evaluating, analyzing, inferring). The concept of *capacity* assumes that the cognitive abilities can be developed. Cognitive functions are not mutually exclusive of emotions. Each is part of a system of biochemically interdependent responses incorporated into one singular system (Damasio, 1994). Cognitive Coaching addresses the intertwined nature of the cognitive and affective systems. Leaders who are coached have an increased capacity for complex thinking and for addressing their own emotions and those of others. Cognitive Coaching draws on the research on teacher cognition and supports increased capacity for planning, reflecting, and problem-resolving. Cognitive Coaching also supports the development of emotional intelligence in principals (Goleman, McKee, & Boyatzis, 2002). Goleman et al. define emotional intelligence as including the following:

- The ability to be conscious about naming one's emotions and connecting to how those emotions influence internal processing and behavior

- Confidence in one's ability to monitor and manage one's emotions

- The capacity to develop emotions that serve to support productive living

- The ability to read the emotions of others and be responsive to them

The mission of Cognitive Coaching expands the traditional work of a leader to include developing cognitive and emotional capacities within others. When principals are coached, they have a richer understanding of how to develop those capacities in teachers, and they simultaneously have their own cognitive and affective capacities expanded.

The mission of Cognitive Coaching describes cognitive capacity as a means for high performance in two domains: independently and in community. Cognitive Coaching draws on the concept of *holonomy*, the study of wholeness (Costa & Garmston, 2002). Central to the mission is a focus on the duality of human existence. Each of us lives an autonomous life with our own thoughts and emotions, unique talents and skills, and a personality unlike anyone else's. Simultaneously, we live as members of systems, such as family systems or organizational systems. We are influenced by the systems in which we live and concurrently, as individuals, influence the systems. The self and the system are interconnected, interdependent, and inseparable. However, the dual nature of this reality creates tension between our internal self and the systems self. Those tensions have been defined as the following tensions of holonomy (Costa & Lipton, 1996):

- Ambiguity and Certainty
- Knowledge and Action
- Egocentricity and Allocentricity
- Self-Assertion and Integration
- Inner Feelings and Outer Behaviors
- Solitude and Interconnectedness

In striving for holonomy, each of us must learn to manage the imbalance created by competing needs. As humans, we naturally seek the equilibrium that comes from certainty. As we traverse the world, we seek out data that confirms our biases and supports our understandings. Simultaneously we have a natural sense of wonder that causes us to seek new learning and drives us to consider our world in new ways that challenge our habitual ways of knowing. The balance between ambiguity and uncertainty is always moving, depending on our current experiences.

Knowledge and action are often incongruent, creating internal pressures. We understand the nature of nutrition and health and yet our eating habits often don't reflect our understanding. In schools, we often violate well-understood principles of learning in our actions. We are hardwired for egocentricity; it provides an internal focus on our own well-being and supports our basic survival. Allocentricity points us outward, focusing us on the perspectives of others. It allows us to collaborate, assess the needs of others, and serve purposes beyond ourselves. The challenge of this tension is the challenge of self and other—when do we go inward and when do we go outward?

Closely aligned with egocentricity and allocentricity is the ability to manage the struggle to know when to self-assert, to speak of one's own needs, and when to defer to others in order to integrate into the group's needs. Our inner thoughts and feelings often differ from our visible behaviors. What we think and what we say are not always congruent. Each of us does a daily dance within our minds about how much of our true inner world to reveal through our words and actions. A final tension occurs between our pull to seek solitude in our own world and thoughts while finding richer meaning and purpose through our interconnectedness.

Resolving some of the tensions allows us to rise to the challenges of human growth and development and to live more productive lives, serving others and ourselves. Through Cognitive Coaching, principals become more skillful in resolving the inherent tensions within themselves and their jobs. The Cognitive Coach is intentional in providing assistance in finding resources to balance and manage the tensions.

Assumptions of Cognitive Coaching

Cognitive Coaching is grounded in the assumption that humans seek learning and growth as inherent parts of their being. It presumes resourcefulness and sufficiency in others. Cognitive Coaching is a process that provides conditions for maximizing the individual's drive for self-directedness.

One of the author's grandsons illustrated this drive in his toddler years. The grandmother was observing her young grandson struggle with a puzzle. Wanting to see him succeed, she offered her assistance. In his innocent way, with his limited language, he responded to her offer with these words, "Grandma, I do it I-self." What a powerful spoken message early in life about the natural drive to be self-directed! The author wisely listened to her grandson's words and backed away, observing him work tirelessly to make the puzzle pieces fit. After much ado, he had some successes and some frustration with the more complex aspects of the puzzle. As he reached the point of maximum effort with low success, he shifted his posture with his grandmother by saying, "Grandma, I need some help." This story illustrates the faith in human capacity within Cognitive Coaching. We are naturally self-directed, striving for a sense of freedom as a learner. We are equally dependent on our environment to support our need to go beyond our current capacity. Cognitive Coaching allows for the human nature within us to find its place in a nurturing environment. It provides support for managing the tensions of autonomy and community.

Cognitive Coaching is a mental model for cognitive development. It assumes that when thinking is mediated, cognitive growth will occur. The word *mediation* is derived from "middle," like the word *median*. The mediator, using a set of coaching skills, intervenes between a person and a task or between a person and an experience. When a person faces a task or problem to be solved, the mediator/coach uses Cognitive Coaching maps and tools to assist the person in thinking clearly about his or her goals and resources. In mediating between a person and an experience, the coach assists the person in reflecting on available data about the experience, analyzing the meaning of the information, and constructing new learning that will lead the person to future applications. The same process occurs in reflection. The coach intervenes between the person and the experience and invites analysis and new insight. From the reflection, the leader is able to project the learnings into future applications.

The intention of the coach is to assist the learner in clarifying, developing, and modifying his or her internal schema (Costa & Garmston, 2002). That is the process for creation of new learning. Without the mediation of thinking, there is little likelihood that internal thought structures will be modified. Consider the effects of a sterile, unmediated environment on a child's development. How have we come to create systems for principals that leave them isolated and unsupported without systems in place to mediate their thinking?

Robert Kegan's constructive-developmental theory

(Drago-Severson, 2004; Kegan, 1995) give insight into how the processes of Cognitive Coaching influence adult development. The theory operates on a fundamental assumption that growth and development are processes that are ongoing and never-ending throughout life. If those growth processes are to be sustained, interventions to reshape and expand internal meaning-making structures are necessary. Kegan differentiates informational learning from transformational learning. Informational learning adds value to what one knows and the skills one can demonstrate. Transformational learning changes the way a person knows. As ways of knowing shift, a leader develops in the ability to deal with greater complexities and challenges in the environment. Kegan names three stages of adult development, sometimes given different names: the socializing, the self-authoring, and the self-transformational (Table 2-1).

Adults at the socializing level can be characterized as dependent on others as a source of their values. Experiences are tests of whether others value them. The environment is the source of well-being. Criticism and conflict are perceived as negative and become threatening to the self. Transition to the self-authoring level is evidenced by a stronger sense of values being internally developed, and an internal set of standards becomes a measuring tool for success. Self-authoring people constantly question whether they are living in a way that is congruent with their own values. The self-transformational adult is most capable of dealing with the world as non-linear, ever-changing, and highly demanding. Conflict is an inherent part of life and is seen as a source of deeper understanding and improvement. Most adults never reach the stage of becoming self-transforming. They remain trapped in earlier stages because they are not in an environment that mediates their development; instead it only adds skills and information to their repertoire.

Table 2-1. Kegan's Stages of Adult Development

Socializing	Self-Authoring	Self-Transforming
• Older adolescents and most adults	• Less than 50% of adults	• Very few adults, usually only after age 40
• Can internalize feelings of others and are guided by them	• Have developed an internal set of rules	• See beyond the limits of their own internal systems
• Able to abstract and respond to needs other than their own	• Internal governing system for decision making and conflict resolution	• See gray as opposed to black and white
• Expectations of others define wants	• Not dependent on others for evaluation and esteem	• Devoted to something beyond themselves
• Entirely reliant on others because they are made up of those around them	• Self-guided, self-evaluative, self-motivated	• See complexity and look across systems
• Ideal for tribal village model where stability and loyalty to the group is first and foremost	• Ideal for a diverse and mobile world focused on ideas, science, freedom, and truth. There are no heroes, only a search for self and self-direction.	• Open to reconstructing what seemed clear
		• Ideal for a world that rejects objectivity and embraces subjectivity, complexity, chaos, and interactive systems

Kegan assists us in having mental models for promoting transformational development. Like children, adults need an environment that provides developmentally appropriate supports while simultaneously offering challenges. It is the critical combination of support and challenge that allows the adult to construct new ways of being and knowing. Without that environment, the conditions for development are nonexistent. Cognitive Coaching is a perfect match to developmental constructivism. It supports teachers and principals with a listening, nonjudgmental ear. It also invites inquiry, a reshaping and reconstructing of one's thinking, and challenges the deep structures of a person's mental models, beliefs, values, and identity. Without this kind of intervention, principals become trapped in a professional development and support system that is informational only. True growth is limited rather than expanded. Cognitive Coaching can create conditions for transformational learning.

Cognitive Coaching is a constructivist model of learning. It rejects behaviorist notions that ignore the capacity of the human mind to create knowledge, examine the meaning of knowledge, and make decisions about how to act on knowledge.

The coach intentionally structures human interactions to maximize productive analysis of one's work and environment in order to act more effectively as a professional. The assumptions of constructivism are as follows:

1. Knowledge is always tentative and incomplete.

2. Knowledge is a personal construction. Everything we know, we have made.

3. Knowledge is a social construction.

4. What learners bring to the learning process matters.

5. Constructivist teaching practices must include shaping the learning environment, activating prior knowledge, social interaction, making meaning of new experiences, and reflecting on new learning.

As professionals, we have a responsibility to those we serve to be continuously learning. There is ample evidence (Joyce & Showers, 2002) to indicate that without coaching, educators have little likelihood of moving knowledge learned in training into important arenas of application. Cognitive Coaching is grounded in the assumption that explicit processes are required to facilitate learning. Learning is not linear, but it is also not haphazard. Attention to structures and processes for learning enhance the likelihood of results and the capacity for forward momentum.

Cognitive Coaching is a nonjudgmental process. The person being coached makes his or her own judgments. The coach builds trust by being nonjudgmental. The coaching environment frees the principal to take risks and examine long-held assumptions without fear. Cognitive Coaching is congruent with the body of research describing the importance of environmental conditions for thoughtful practice. Under stress, the brain reverts to old pathways that move the actor toward fight or flight. Those patterns are counterproductive for the conditions and needs of today's principals. In contrast, Cognitive Coaching enhances the environmental conditions necessary to sustain the neural capacity to work at the neocortical, or higher level thinking, part of the brain. If we want principals to be thoughtful, reflective practitioners, we have a responsibility to provide systems of support to make that happen. The skills of the Cognitive Coach enhance and support the most basic neural needs in order to develop our most exquisite capacities.

Four Support Functions

Costa and Garmston (2002) have developed a model of four functions for professional support: Cognitive Coaching, collaborating, consulting, and evaluating. These functions allow those who are supporting principals to be clear about the purpose of their interactions and to apply functions to their work based on need rather than some prescribed process. Costa and Garmston refer to it as a capability: "Know one's intentions and choose congruent behaviors." All four support functions are intended to support growth and development, but they do so in very different ways. All four have a place in principal support systems. Evaluating is probably the most familiar in educational settings. It refers to making judgments about a principal's performance based on a well-understood set of external standards. Although principal evaluation is an important accountability measure for districts, it has little potential for transformational growth because it is externally imposed and rarely constructivist in nature. The implementation most often relates to personnel systems rather than growth.

Consulting is also a familiar form of support in the world of schools. Consultants work to support principals by providing expertise and knowledge to them with the intention to expand their informational learning. This is often seen in the form of mentor programs, in which retired principals are assigned to active principals to share their knowledge and experiences. The mentors help the principals "learn the job" and problem-solve with them. Though very helpful, without an added Cognitive Coaching component, these are not effective in transformational learning, the most effective source of adult development.

Collaborating creates a team or a pair of principals to plan, problem-solve, or inquire. Collaboration involves a community of learners sharing their ideas and creating learning together. This has been shown to be a very effective strategy for principal professional development (Drago-Severson, 2004). In her research on 25 principals, Drago-Severson found that 24 wanted reflective dialogue with their colleagues, but they were not making that part of their practice. The challenges of creating professional learning communities for teachers are well known; the challenges for principals might be even greater given time demands and logistical issues of geographical distance.

Coaching has the greatest potential for transformational learning. It is an ongoing process in which the coach invites regular reflection based on the needs of the principal. It supports the principal by developing increased capacity with the principal's internal resources. It is a constructivist-developmental process, one of the most compatible of the four support functions with transformational learning. Coaching also has challenges in terms of resources and time, which will be addressed later in the book.

A key feature that differentiates the four support functions is the source of judgment in each. In Cognitive Coaching, the judgments are made by the principal: "I was not happy with the meeting today because . . . " In collaborating, the judgments are shared by the collaborators: "We seem to agree that by disaggregating our data, we are becoming more effective in addressing learner deficits." Consulting provides judgments about the criteria for performance using the consultant's expertise to define them: "When you can document that you are spending 30% of your time on learning walks, you can expect to see some gains from the process." In evaluating, the criteria are set through defined standards, and the evaluator makes judgments about the principal's performance in relation to the data: "Your work is a level 3 on our performance criteria for instructional leadership. Here are the data I am using to make that rating."

Five States of Mind

Cognitive Coaching draws on an impressive list of many well-respected researchers, including Lev Vygotsky, Richard Bandler and John Grinder, Carl Jung, Richard Shavelson, David Berliner, Carl Glickman, Arthur Koestler, Reuven Feuerstein, Albert Bandura, Gregory Bateson, Noam Chomsky, John Dewey, Robert Goldhammer and Morris Cogan, Antonio Damasio, Carl Rogers, and Abraham Maslow. At the core of the work, and unique to this model, is the concept of States of Mind; this is the original work of Costa and Garmston. The States of Mind describe and illuminate the resources necessary to become intentionally holonomous and self-directed. They are abstractions that provide a conceptual framework for understanding the internal drives within each of us. The five States of Mind that are central to the work of a Cognitive Coach are efficacy, flexibility, consciousness, craftsmanship, and interdependence.

Efficacy

Teacher and school efficacy are among the most highly researched topics of educational literature. Albert Bandura (1997) described self-efficacy as the "belief in one's capabilities to organize and execute the courses of action required to produce given attainments." In an educational setting, efficacy is an internally held sense that one has the knowledge and skills to impact the learning processes in the school to attain the desired results. Efficacy exists within individuals and for schools. With high efficacy, a principal knows that his or her actions make a difference across the school community. Each interaction contributes to the overall learning of the community. High teacher efficacy means that teachers hold a belief that their actions will result in student learning. Ongoing efforts will pay off with results. When a person has low efficacy, there is a strong external locus of control, often manifesting itself as blame and victimization: "These kids come from such deprived homes," or "I had such better results when I had a different population of students."

Efficacy is a foundational State of Mind, a resource that gives us motivation, hope, and belief in our own ability to influence and change our world. Research on efficacy (Tschannen-Moran, Woolfolk-Hoy, & Hoy, 1998) has shown the following:

- Efficacy is self-fulfilling. With increased efficacy, teachers make a greater effort, leading to improved results. With lower efficacy, less effort is expended, leading to fewer positive results.

- Efficacy leads to openness, new ideas, and experimentation to support learning.
- Efficacy increases resilience and the willingness to persist in efforts in the face of challenges.
- Efficacy decreases criticism of students when they are not successful and increases their planning and organizational skills.
- Efficacy decreases the likelihood a teacher will make a special education referral.
- Efficacy increases a teacher's enthusiasm for teaching.
- Efficacy at the school level relates to a healthy organizational climate.
- School efficacy relates to an orderly and positive environment and more classroom-based decision making.

Consciousness

Consciousness leads to self-awareness and allows for the examination of other States of Mind. It requires attention to one's own metacognition. Highly conscious principals listen to their own listening. In working with others, they notice the biases that interfere with their ways of understanding, they think about how their preferences affect their perceptions, and they track the processes of their thinking. They ask themselves the following questions:

- Am I being logical or emotional?
- How is my prior knowledge of this situation affecting my thought processes?
- What judgments am I making?
- How can I gain another perspective on this?
- What might I do to become more data-based?

These are examples of the kinds of internal questions a conscious person would ask. Such consciousness provides capacity for reflection before, during, and after an experience.

In addition to paying internal attention, the conscious leader monitors external cues and data in an ongoing manner. In working with a teacher, the principal pays attention to the subtle nonverbal cues in addition to the words being spoken. The principal who observes a classroom is aware of the need to attend to both the teachers and the learners. Focus is given to both types of data. Every experience is lived at two levels: attention to self and attention to others. The executive capacity to manage both simultaneously is a sign of a highly developed consciousness. The conscious person also makes connections between past and present experiences, seeking patterns and connections. The ability to do that kind of thinking is what distinguishes us from other mammals (Damasio, 1994).

Craftsmanship

Craftsmanship is an internal drive toward personal and group excellence. It manifests itself behaviorally in a drive for continual improvement. It is not about becoming a perfectionist, but about focusing on clear criteria for quality. It is about measuring one's performance against a standard and seeking ongoing means for moving toward a higher standard. Craftsmanship is data-driven. Principals with high craftsmanship invite the use of data in determining areas of growth for their schools. They push the envelope and invite shared dissatisfaction with the current state, always holding higher and higher expectations for students and staff. They model their value of growth in their actions and expectations. They commend success by giving specific feedback on the sources and examples of striving for higher performance. Simultaneously, they support analysis of cause and effect and assist staff in setting future goals. Craftsmanship is not judgmental but seeks ongoing self-assessment using criteria for excellence. From the self-assessment stage, craftsmanship leads us to examine our actions and their outcomes, with an intention to refine them for development and growth toward even more successful performance and outcomes.

Flexibility

Flexibility is the State of Mind that allows us to move beyond our natural tendency toward egocentricity. Egocentricity is necessary for survival; it allows us to monitor our internal states, knowing when to withdraw from a situation and even telling us when we need to take shelter and food. However, egocentricity simultaneously limits our ability to see and understand our world beyond our internal framework and lense. Low flexibility is the source of low creativity and high rigidity. We are trapped by our egocentricity, becoming blind to new and different ways of seeing. Margaret Wheatley (2005) describes listening for flexibility as follows:

> There are many ways to sit and listen for the differences. Lately, I've been listening for what surprises me. What did I just hear that startled me? This isn't easy—I'm accustomed to sit there nodding my head as someone voices what I agree with. But when I notice what surprises me, I'm able to see my own views more clearly, including my beliefs and assumptions. (p. 212)

Flexible principals are open to understanding the multiple perspectives of their staff and embracing the diversity. As Wheatley (2005) states, "It's not the differences that divide us. It's our judgments that do. Curiosity and good listening bring us back together" (p. 212). Taking those multiple perspectives enhances a leader's ability to unite diverse factions. Flexibility is a doorway to interdependence.

Flexibility is also a touchstone for creativity and problem solving. A flexible principal explores multiple alternatives, viewpoints, and possibilities. We spoke with a participant in Tennessee whose school was struggling with tardiness. Many efforts had been tried, including student consequences and appeals to parents. Thinking flexibly, the principal purchased alarm clocks for students and distributed them while talking about self-management and self-monitoring. Behaviors began to change. The flexible position moved from blaming and punishing to inviting alternative behaviors.

Interdependence

Interdependence is a resource that allows us to move beyond a self-centered view of the world to a view that assists us in seeing ourselves as part of something larger. Interdependence helps us to move among egocentricity (self-centeredness), allocentricity (other-centeredness), and macrocentricity (system-centeredness). Interdependence draws on our ability to see the nature of our relationships instead of thinking in isolation. Wheatley (2005) notes the following:

> Those of us educated in Western culture learned to think and manage a world that was anything but systemic or interconnected. It's a world of separations and clear boundaries: jobs in boxes, lines delineating relationships, roles, and policies describing what each individual does and who we expect them to be. (p. 100)

> The recognition that individuals need each other lies at the heart of every system. From that realization, individuals reach out, and seemingly divergent self-interests develop into a system of interdependency. Thus, all systems form through collaboration, from the recognition that we need another in order to survive. (p. 102)

Mutuality and reciprocity are critical attributes of interdependence. Interdependent people see themseves inside a system and appreciate the flow of resources. They understand the need to contribute to the system and appreciate the value they receive from the system.

Given the growing body of research on the importance of building collaborative cultures in order to impact student achievement, effective principals will move beyond a hierarchal and authoritarian structure of leadership. In order to do so, they will need to have their own internal resource of high interdependence with the staff and the school district. They will also need to have a skill set for creating increasing interdependencies within the school. Table 2-2 sums up the characteristics of the five States of Mind.

Table 2-2. Key Characteristics of the States of Mind

EFFICACY

Having internal resourcefulness	Initiating responsibility	Knowing one has choices and making choices	Being a problem solver	Taking action

CONSCIOUSNESS

Being aware of self, others, and the setting	Knowing about one's thinking	Seeking data about self, others, and the setting	Being aware of one's own and others' styles and preferences	Monitoring one's own decisions and the effects

CRAFTSMANSHIP

Being intentional	Striving for improvement and refinement	Seeking clarity and precision	Assessing for excellence	Pursuing ongoing learning

cont.

FLEXIBILITY

Seeking generating alternatives	Seeing multiple perspect-ives	Being willing to consider change	Adjusting to others' styles and preferences	Tolerating ambiguity

INTERDEPENDENCE

Contribut-ing to the common good	Participat-ing with and learn-ing from others	Developing capacity in interacting with others	Seeking collegiality and collabor-ation	Balanc-ing self needs and group needs

How does a coach utilize the knowledge of the States of Mind to support self-directed learning? Cognitive coaches listen closely to the thoughts of the coachee. As they listen, they hear the content of the words being delivered. At a deeper level, they listen for what the words say about the person's States of Mind. Consider the following example:

> *Principal*: I have been working with this team for 2 years now. I've been patient with them because I know they are working with very challenging con-ditions. They have a very high number of at-risk kids and have had a lot of turnover of both students and staff. Yet I am seeing little progress in student achievement or team functioning. I have tried the same things I have done with other teams that have been successful, but I don't see it making any differ-ence here. I don't think I have been an effective leader with them because I can't seem to facilitate change in the current conditions.

An astute coach will hear, first and foremost, low effi-cacy. This principal is used to successfully facilitating team growth and development. In spite of her best efforts, she is seeing little change. She expresses frustration with her ability to lead and feels powerless to make a difference. She is highly conscious. She is aware of the work she has done, the assumptions she has made, and the differences in her effects compared to other teams. Although she generally has strategies for her work with teams, her craftsmanship is low in this situation because she has exhausted her ways of working effectively. Although she is striving for excellence, she is unable to draw on her internal resources to find alternative ways of working. The principal is alone in her efforts, not seeking resources beyond herself or asking the team for assistance. Interdependence is not obvious in her words, nor is flexibility. She sees few alternatives and is not taking a perspective other than her own as a frustrated principal.

A coach for this principal would do well to begin with her strong consciousness as a gateway into the other States of Mind. Some possible questions might be the following:

- What are you aware of about your own patterns and choices in supporting this team?

- What are the key questions you think you need to address with this team?

- What specific things in your work seem to be most distressing to you as a leader?

After pursuing that line of questioning, the coach might find other entry points for supporting the principal's craftsmanship and efficacy:

- What are some of your key leverage points with this team?

- What are some specific areas of collaboration you'd like to see?

- When you work with a challenge, what do you most often do to attack it in a strategic manner?

- What are some things you might not be seeing in this situation?

As the coach asks these questions, the thinking of the principal deepens, expands, and takes on new dimensions. The direction is unknown to the coach because the new thinking is created inside the principal. The coach deftly uses States of Mind as a means to create new possibilities, new thinking, and new resources.

Coaching Conversation Maps

Cognitive Coaching is guided by three conversation maps. A map is a symbolic representation of some territory we might like to explore. It serves as a guide for assisting us through some terrain, helping us to stay on course and get where we want to go. We know that the map is only a depiction and that we have to make midcourse corrections as we traverse the territory. Cognitive Coaching maps serve a similar function. They give us templates for conversations for planning, reflecting, and problem resolving. They are not scripts, but guides through the territory of the teacher's and principal's thinking. They serve to focus the conversation, keeping it on course and supporting the productive use of time. The maps reflect research on effective planning, reflecting, and problem resolving. As coaches internalize the maps, it frees them to focus fully on truly listening to the internal maps of the teacher's and principal's minds, revealed in their conversations. Furthermore, it guides the coach in patterns of questioning that build a capacity for self-directed learning. The Cognitive Coaching model is based on three maps, each with a different purpose.

The Planning Conversation Map (Table 2-3) assists a principal or teacher in preparing for an upcoming event. It is generic and can be used for multiple purposes (e.g., planning a staff meeting, preparing for a parent conference, long-range planning related to school improvement). This map has two focuses in assisting a principal in preparation: the event and the person doing the planning. It ends with a reflection on the coaching.

Table 2-3. The Planning Conversation Map

Region	Sample Questions
Clarify goals	What are some things you hope to accomplish in this meeting? What outcomes are you considering in planning for this meeting?
Specify success indicators and a plan for collecting evidence	What are some ways you will be assessing your outcomes? What are some things you will be monitoring as indicators that you are achieving your goals? What data might you collect related to your targets?
Anticipate approaches, strategies, decisions, and a plan to monitor them	What are some of the specific components you are considering for the meeting? What things might be important to do, given your audience? What are some things that you might be paying attention to as the meeting progresses? What are some of the decisions you might anticipate making as the meeting progresses? How will you know?
Establish personal learning focus and processes for self-assessment	What do you want to be conscious of in yourself as the meeting progresses? How will you monitor that? What do you hope to learn as a result of this meeting that will support your future work? What is most challenging for you in thinking about conducting this meeting?

cont.

Reflect on the coaching process and explore refinements	How has our time together assisted you in feeling prepared for this meeting? What is clearer for you after thinking together about this meeting? What feedback might you offer about our work together?

The first three regions of the map focus on the event. Here the principal has the opportunity to mentally rehearse the event, gaining greater clarity and craftsmanship about the event's desired outcomes and the ways of assessing those outcomes. The principal anticipates effective strategies and considers ways to monitor and adjust as the event progresses.

The fourth region, the personal learning focus, shifts the principal's thinking from the event to an internal focus. The principal is asked to identify areas of learning and growth. This region may be the most critical region of the map because it is the source of an internal focus and goal setting for learning. Without this element, the map is shallow, providing only thinking for the event, but no deeper commitment to professional growth and meaning-making from the experience.

The fifth region of the map invites reflection on the conversation, providing thinking for synthesis to the principal and feedback to the coach.

The Reflecting Conversation Map (Table 2-4) serves the principal in analyzing and learning from experiences. It invites a person to move from a significant experience to making meaning of the experience in a manner that leads to transferring learning into the future. Without reflection, principals are doomed to repeat patterns of behavior. In contrast to the common educational practice of planning, few educators are given the opportunity to reflect, and few have internalized the processes of reflection. This

Table 2-4. The Reflecting Conversation Map

Region	Sample Questions
Summarize impressions and recall supporting information	How are you feeling about the meeting? How do you think it went? What causes you to think that? On what information are you basing that?
Analyze causal factors	How did the meeting go compared to how you envisioned it? What were you aware of about the decisions you were making during the meeting? What do you think might have been going on for others in the meeting? What was going on for you internally when . . . ? How did you know to . . . ?
Construct new learning	What are some things you are more aware of in your planning as a result of your experience? What are some things you are learning about yourself? What are you learning about this kind of meeting? What are you taking away from this experience?
Commit to application	When might you apply these insights in similar meetings? How does this experience inform you for the future? What commitments might you make to yourself based on this experience?
Reflect on the coaching process and explore refinements	How has our conversation supported your thinking? What about our time together has been most useful to you?

map provides a structure that moves principals and teachers from focusing on events (episodic thinking) to gleaning key learnings and generalizations from experiences. In this way the map is compatible with how human brains remember. We do not remember specifics, but instead store generalizations and guiding principles (e.g., Inclusion is a key factor in decision making, budgeting is something that is often misunderstood by staff). Those larger frames inform us in the future. Smaller frames (e.g., That was a challenging staff meeting because three teachers were upset about how the final decision was made), do not inform us for the future. They only cause us to repeatedly recycle an event.

In the Reflecting Conversation, the coach is careful not to invite storytelling, a simple reiteration of the experience. Instead the coach supports the principal in linking impressions with data that support those impressions. The critical focus of this map is on analyzing causal factors. The coach supports high principal and teacher consciousness by assisting the thinking about each decision and each part of the experience. As those are analyzed, the principal begins to construct new learning about factors that contributed to the outcomes, successes, and/or failures in the experience. From that analysis, the principal is able to gain new insights that lead to generalizations for future application. The final region of the map, reflecting on the process, is the same as in the Planning Conversation.

The Problem-Resolving Map (Figure 2-1) draws on brain research about the human mind under stress. It is a map a coach might use with a principal or teacher who is seemingly low in resources and unable to find a forward direction. Examples might be the following:

- A principal or teacher is uncertain about how to implement a new program.

- A principal or teacher is having a difficult relationship with an assistant.

- A difficult parent issue seems without resolution.
- The pressure to deliver improved test scores discourages a principal or teacher.

The Problem-Resolving Map differs from the other maps in that it is more conceptual and less focused on specific steps to explore. The States of Mind are the source of questions in all three maps but are especially critical in this map. The coach is attuned to the emotional and cognitive needs of the coachee, balancing the two.

Figure 2-1. The Problem-Resolving Map

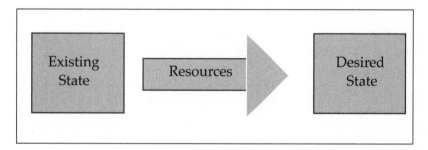

The map first attends to an acknowledgement of the existing state—that is, the current reality for the coachee. This is important because, under threat, the brain experiences neurochemical changes that cause a loss of cognitive capacity. The structure and processes of the map support enhanced cognition. The map begins with a process called pacing, which paraphrases the existing state and frames the desired state of the person. Attention is given to both the emotion and the content of the existing state (e.g., You're hurt because your boss is not seeing your contributions).

The map's structure leads the coach to refocus the coachee's energy toward the desired state. The coachee begins to envision a better future (e.g., feeling valued). The increase in the brain's neurotransmitters occurs when language is given to create an image of something more positive. The coach uses language to assist the problem-resolver in expressing a more desirable way of being.

Finally, using the States of Mind as sources of energy, the coach questions the problem-resolver to develop internal resources related to the desired state.

Skilled coaches develop flexibility in using the maps. They sometimes use only some of the regions of a map in their mediation of the principal's thinking. Other times they modify the sequencing of the maps to align its regions with the needs of the principal. Coaches use the maps both formally and informally. A short conversation in the hall might cover just a few elements of a map, and the coach (C) could leave the principal (P) with a question to think about, as in the following dialogue:

> *A short conversation in the hall might cover just a few elements of the map, and the coach could leave the principal with a question to think about.*

P: I can't talk long because I have an important meeting to go to with a parent. It's not going to be an easy one.

C: You're worried about this meeting being especially challenging.

P: Yes, it will be.

C: What are your goals for the meeting?

P: I want to find out what the parents' real concerns are. We seem to get frequent criticism, but I don't know what the real issues are.

C: So you want to clarify the focus of their anxiety.

P: Yes.

C: What would you like to leave the meeting with?

P: That's a helpful question. I think I want to have a specific list of concerns that we can begin to tackle, one by one.

C: So you have a target now. As you leave, what are

you thinking about as actions you will take in the meeting to be certain you leave with the list?

P: I'll be thinking about that as I go to the meeting.

The conversation did not bring closure to the principal's planning for the meeting. The brief hallway conversation is still coaching, however, and leaves the principal more resourceful. The coach knows that it will be possible to work with the principal around challenging parent meetings in future conversations. The focus of coaching is on serving the needs of the person in the moment, not on completing the maps.

Skilled coaches make conscious decisions about which maps to use, even switching between maps during a conversation. The effective coach enters a conversation listening to the principal's words. The words guide the coach's decision making about which map to use. Consider the following example:

P: I'd like to talk with you about the staff meeting next week, when we will be doing some analysis of the recent results of our state tests.

C: You'd like to think through the best way to support teachers in using this new information.

P: That would be helpful.

C: What are some things you hope to accomplish in this meeting?

P: Well, I want a celebration of our gains, but simultaneously some acceptance of some of the less positive results.

C: So you hope to develop some ownership of the results, both positive and negative.

P: Yes, and I want a balance of the two.

C: What would you expect to hear in the meeting or observe that would tell you that teachers are feeling ownership of student learning results?

P: That's exactly my struggle. Every time we talk about test scores, I get a launching of emotions and a big whine about how unfair it is to do this to us. I am exhausted by it and so tired of the repeated pattern; I just can't seem to stop the spin.

C: You're tired of the same old behaviors and very uncertain about how to break the pattern in your staff.

P: That's so true. It seems so dramatic. I just wish I could move this forward instead of constantly revisiting the same old issues.

C: What you want is to be a leader of renewed energy and vision around student learning.

P: Exactly!

C: I'm going to leave you with a question that I don't want you to answer now. Just think about it and we'll talk again. What might be some indicators of a staff with renewed energy?

The coach began the conversation with the intention to support the principal's planning. The principal established his goals for the meeting, the first region of the planning map. When the coach asked him to describe his success indicators, the principal became emotional and expressed his strong frustration. The coach heard the frustration and moved to a different map, the Problem-Resolving Map. The coach paraphrased for the existing state and followed that with a paraphrase for the principal's desired state. This is the way a Cognitive Coach thinks, always monitoring the needs and meaning of the coachee's words. That information becomes a source for the coach's decisions about how to proceed and which map to use. This is the art of coaching.

Coaching Tools

Cognitive Coaches work from a tool kit of effective communication skills that support creating an environment of trust. If the principal is to grow transformation-ally, there must be challenge and support. The coach's tool kit is congruent with those intentions. One principal called the coaching sessions a "brain massage." In a skilled mas-sage, there is an opportunity to tune out other stimuli and focus on oneself. The atmosphere is relaxed and slowed in pace. However, with deep massage, like deep thinking, there is often some pain and challenge.

Rapport skills allow the coach to create comfort in the moment and let the principal know that the coach is truly present and listening intently. The kind of listening that is apparent when the coach attends fully, using verbal and nonverbal skills, is rarely seen in a principal's day. The rap-port is intended to create optimal conditions for thinking.

Cognitive Coaches are knowledgeable in behaviors designed to mediate thinking. Those behaviors include pausing, paraphrasing, and probing for specificity. Our culture has come to equate speed with intelligence. Similarly, we equate productivity with speed (Wheatley, 2005). The pause provides time to think for both the coach and the principal. It allows space to engage in the behaviors of com-plex thinking and reflection. Pausing has been shown to create an increased level of cognitive functioning in students. It is our experience that the same is true for adult learners.

> *Cognitive Coaches are knowl-edgeable in behaviors designed to mediate thinking.*

Paraphrasing, well executed, is a fundamental tool for mediating thinking. When principals hear their own words reflected back in a rephrased manner, it is often the first time that they attend to the meaning of their own thinking. The social construction of placing one's thinking between the coach and the principal, examining it with one's own words, and then examining it a second time through the coach's paraphrases causes a reshaping and deeper examination of the internal thought processes that might have been unexpressed. Without language being put to the inner thoughts, they remain inaccessible and cannot be modified. Cognitive Coaches use a variety of paraphrasing types to cause principals to hear their own feelings, key concepts, and generalizations. The most complex paraphrases give the principal access to his or her inner beliefs, values, assumptions, goals, and mental models.

Probing for specificity is one way that a coach increases the principal's precision and craftsmanship. Words are simply an externalization of thinking. When words lack specificity, it is often a reflection of a lack of clarity in thinking. Take, for instance, a principal who says, "It's important to me that my teachers collaborate." If the principal is to genuinely target teacher collaboration, she will need to have a clear picture of the meaning of collaboration. Does it mean that teachers share texts? Co-plan? Examine student work? Use common assessments? The Cognitive Coach would assist the principal in moving toward clarity by replying with a probe such as "If your teachers were genuinely collaborating, what are some of the behaviors you might expect to see?" Another probe might be "What does collaboration mean to you?" Probes bring focus and clarity to words and allow us to move them to action.

Inquiry is another tool a coach uses. Inquiry differs from probing in that it has the intention to broaden thinking rather than focus it. The coach, speaking to the principal about the value of collaboration, could inquire, "What do you anticipate happening for students if teachers were to collaborate?" or "As you envision a more collaborative school, what downsides might there be?" Effective inquiry is open ended and has no agenda. It is an invitation to explore. Inquiry has an intellectual risk embedded in it: It can cause me to think about things that I had not considered before, or it might make visible things that are uncomfortable, challenging, or even threatening. This is the heart of using Cognitive Coaching for transformational learning. Inquiry moves the principal into the territory of challenge. In pairing inquiry with the other coaching tools, it also creates a sense of support. When principals are invited to think through inquiry, they begin to internalize the process of inquiry and become more self-directed in developing a professional identity as an inquirer.

A Coaching Conversation

Take a moment to consider and analyze the following example of a typical coaching conversation with a principal. As you read, notice how the coach uses a pattern of paraphrasing and questioning. As you explore the conversation, speculate on which of the three conversation maps the coach is using. How might the coach have decided on this map? Read also for the possible States of Mind of the principal. Which seem to be a high resource or a low resource?

C: I'm looking forward to working with you this year. How are things going so far?

P: Being new to this school, I'm working hard to listen, and I'm finding the school to be so very different from my last experience.

C: You're noticing some things you didn't anticipate.

P: That's true.

C: What are some of the differences you are observing?

P: There seems to be some hesitation to work in teams. I even heard one teacher say that she didn't like to share her ideas with others because the kids would not find them new and fresh when she used them.

C: You've discovered that collaboration is not a norm here, and there is even some resistance to the concept of teachers sharing best practices.

P: Yes, and it concerns me because we have so many

new teachers in the building who need to learn from the veterans.

C: It's important to you that teachers support one another and learn from one another.

P: Very much so.

C: As you analyze the situation, what do you think is the source of the reluctance to share?

P: I've interviewed several members of the staff and need to interview more. I don't have enough information yet to make a judgment, but it seems to be an issue of trust. I don't see much team planning going on, and some teachers seem very isolated. Some of the staff have told me that there are some members who intimidate others.

C: So you've gathered some data from the staff, but you're not sure you have adequate facts to make conclusions yet.

P: I need to hear from others still.

C: Based on the information you have, what are some patterns you are beginning to see?

P: Well, there seem to be haves and have-nots. I hadn't thought of it before, but even the most positive folks I've spoken with seem to think that the last principal depended on a few folks, and they got all the rewards.

C: So a concern about fair treatment is emerging.

P: I think that's quite true.

C: What other data might you need to collect to test your hypothesis?

P: *Fairness* is the right word. That seems to capture it. I know that sometimes one small issue can take on a life of its own, such as one teacher going to a conference and others not having the opportunity. It would be useful to collect some history of how decisions about those kinds of rewards are made. I might be able to create some structures that are different and encourage sharing of learning.

C: You're thinking that decision making is a key issue in how people perceive fair treatment. You have some ideas about how you might tackle that issue in a way that could also encourage teachers to share.

P: Yes, I'm comfortable with expecting teachers to share as a contingency for having access to professional development opportunities. I think there are other issues here, but this might be a place to explore the school's climate.

C: You're starting to frame these issues as school culture.

P: Well, maybe that is the issue.

C: What are some things you learned in your last school about developing culture?

P: My last school had a really strong collaborative culture when I came in as principal, and I didn't have to do much other than reinforce it and sustain the structures that were in place.

C: You're learning that you might need to be a different kind of leader in this school and that a focus for you will be developing a stronger culture.

P: I'm beginning to see things in a new light.

C: Where does that take you in your next steps in entering this school?

P: That's a challenging question for me. I'm not sure I know how to do that, given my last experience. I think that is an area where I may need to do some studying. One thing that comes to mind is that I need to think about what I am modeling in each interaction that sends a message about what I expect as a leader of a different culture.

C: Today you are aware that you are going to have to reflect on what you might do to become a different kind of leader. You're clear that the modeling you do on a daily basis will be critical.

P: Yes, that is a place to start.

C: How has our time together supported your thinking about how you want to enter this school?

P: Hearing myself talk about what I have been thinking has solidified what was in my gut and swirling in my head. I think I know more about some things I need to pay more attention to, and I know I need to reflect more on what leadership might look like in this school. I'm not sure I'm ready to formulate any plans, but I know I need to explore the concept of building school culture. I'm grateful for your help in widening my understanding of what I need to pay attention to.

C: Thank you, I'm glad our time has been useful. You're starting to think about who you need to be at this school, in contrast to your last school. We can certainly continue this conversation with that in mind. Let's talk about when we can get together again.

In this conversation, we hear the principal move to deeper insights about his initial learning about his new school. Although the presenting problem seems to be about teaming, the conversation causes the principal to search his data for meaning inside the patterns. He moves deeper in his thinking about his role as a leader and begins to consider his identity in the school. He explores what it means to be a developer of culture and leaves with new questions and new focus.

The coach engaged in a pattern of paraphrasing and questioning typical of skillful coaching. She used a variety of types of paraphrases to mediate the thinking of the principal, carefully reflecting back with different words. The concept labels of *fairness* and *school culture* caused the principal to hear his words in a bigger frame of reference. The questions asked by the coach reflected her listening for the States of Mind of the principal. Table 2-5 codes some examples of what State of Mind the coach was intentionally mediating.

Table 2-5. Mediating States of Mind

Coach's Words	State of Mind
You're noticing some things you didn't anticipate. What are some of the differences you are observing?	Consciousness
As you analyze the situation, what do you think is the source of the reluctance to share?	Flexibility, Consciousness, Craftsmanship
Based on the information you have, what are some patterns are you beginning to see?	Craftsmanship, Consciousness
What are some things you learned in your last school about developing culture?	Efficacy, Flexibility
Where does that take you in your next steps in entering this school?	Craftsmanship, Consciousness

The conversation has not brought closure to the principal's thinking, but it has opened a variety of new pathways to explore. The goal of the coach is to invite ongoing thinking that will support the principal in making choices and taking action based on new insights. The coaching conversation is not one visit or one event, but a beginning of a process of supported thinking.

The Cognitive Coaching Process

Every human interaction is an opportunity to mediate another person's thinking. We do not choose to mediate in every interaction, but the choice is always available. In viewing coaching as ongoing, we begin to view our work as a process of continual improvement and development. Although most principals come to their work with skills, the job is organic, changing, and evolving. Effective administrators seek opportunities to reflect on practice and to broaden and deepen their thinking and internal thought process. Without a coaching process, opportunities for reflection and focused thinking become infrequent. Cognitive Coaching provides a structure for and expectation of reflective practice. Cognitive Coaching is not a process of evaluation. Evaluation exists to make judgments about a principal's performance. It is a key feature of effective human resource management, but it is generally ineffective in developing professionals with increased capacity for rich cognition and self-directedness. Many principals receive infrequent visits from supervisors, often only when there is a crisis. The process of Cognitive Coaching institutionalizes the expectation that principals will be supported as growing professionals.

Why Coaching Principals Is So Important

Time and time again, reference is made to the critical role of the principal in implementing change, keeping a school vision on track, and creating a collaborative culture for teachers and students. There has been little deliberate action to develop principals. Given high accountability and an influx of new and inexperienced principals due to massive retirement, it is time to give more strategic attention to the development of principals. As one principal put it:

> We are asked to sustain others all the time—we need some sustenance too! Sustaining our own health and well-being requires us to give up trying to be all things to all people—after all, everyone has the capacity to be self directed—our role is support them in that. What a weight off our shoulders as principals. The CC [Cognitive Coaching] not only sustains us in our work with others but can assist us professionally as we coach each other.

This book is a call to action around that noble purpose.

Human growth and development is the result of interaction with one's environment. The nature of the environment is critical to the process of development. Isolation, external judgments from others, and authoritarian mandates are not the means for developing high-quality principals. Cognitive Coaching of principals is one process for achieving some different and critical ends for our futures. It is reasonable to ask what outcomes might be anticipated if such a strategic vision is created and sustained. Wheatley (2005, p 215) states it eloquently and succinctly when she says, "Thinking is the place where intelligent action begins."

"Thinking is the place where intelligent action begins."

When principals, like students and teachers, are invited and expected to use their cognitive internal resources to plan, reflect, and problem-resolve, the following behaviors may be predicted (Joyce & Showers, 2002):

- Accelerated professional growth

- Increases in the five States of Mind—efficacy, con-

sciousness, craftsmanship, flexibility, and interdependence
- Reduced stress levels
- Increased job satisfaction
- Higher retention rate in the profession
- Greater impact on teachers' capacities
- A vision of their work as creating transformational learning for the professional development of their teachers
- Increased coaching of teachers
- Increased institutionalization of new practices

New practices are learned and often lost before they become internalized. When principals are coached, the likelihood that new practices will be sustained and institutionalized is increased to statistically significant levels. Given the rate of change and learning in today's educational systems, we must provide structures for assisting principals in becoming more effective and efficient in learning the changing skills required by their profession. Moreover, if Cognitive Coaching is to become everyday practice in schools for all stakeholders, the principals will have to be the chief coaches. Only by becoming skilled models of coaching will they become coaching leaders in their systems.

Schools have focused their energy on classrooms and students. That is well and good; however, this overly simplistic view has missed the importance of looking at the entire system and culture of the organization. Until we make significant changes in the cultures of schools, tinkering with parts of the system will only lead to small gains. We have seen few significant gains in the last decades in student learning. Until we take a larger view of the systems issues in educational organizations, we are likely to repeat our history of ineffectiveness and incremental gains. Cognitive Coaching is not another innovation on our plate; it *is* the plate. As such, it provides an implementation process to support all the innovations. It is a systemic process for transformational learning. Only when the key role of the principal is participating in the transformational learning process can we expect to be renewing, adapting, and growing for the future demands to be faced.

References

Bandura, A. (1997). *Self-efficacy: The exercise of control*. New York: Freeman.

Clark, C., & Peterson, P. (1986). Teachers' thought processes. In M. C. Wittrock (Ed.), *Handbook of research on teaching* (3rd ed). New York: Macmillan.

Costa, A., & Garmston, R. (2002). *Cognitive Coaching: A foundation for renaissance schools*. Norwood, MA: Christopher-Gordon.

Costa, A., & Lipton. L. (1996). *Holonomy: Paradox and promise*. Unpublished article.

Damasio, A. (1994). *Descartes' error: Emotion, reason and the human brain*. New York: HarperCollins.

Drago-Severson, E. (2004). *Helping teachers learn*. Thousand Oaks, CA: Corwin Press.

Ellison, J., & Hayes, C. (2005). *Cognitive Coaching foundation seminar learning guide*. Norwood, MA: Christopher-Gordon.

Goleman, D., McKee, A., & Boyatzis, R. E. (2002). *Primal leadership*. Cambridge, MA: Harvard Business School.

Joyce, B., & Showers, B. (2002). *Student achievement through staff development* (3rd ed.). Alexandria, VA: Association for Supervision and Curriculum Development.

Kegan, R. (1995). *In over our heads: The mental demands of modern life*. Cambridge, MA: Harvard University Press.

Tschannen-Moran, M., Woolfolk-Hoy, A., & Hoy, W. K. (1998). Teacher efficacy: Its meaning and measure. *Review of Educational Research, 68* (2), 202–248.

Wheatley, M. J. (2005). *Finding our way: Leadership for an uncertain time*. San Francisco: Berrett-Koehler.

3

The Effects of Supporting Principals With Cognitive Coaching

What happens when a principal has a regular 30- to 40-minute appointment with a coach? Because coaching emerged as a profession in the 1990s and the focus in education has been on coaching teachers, there is little information in the literature to determine its effect on principals. The coaching of principals is taking place in school districts, but few studies have been conducted.

> The coaching of principals is taking place in school districts, but few studies have been conducted

A recent issue of *Education Leadership* (May 2005) focused on supporting new educators. Of the 18 articles included in the journal, 10 focused on teachers and 8 concerned principals; not one article mentioned coaching. The *Handbook of Research on School Supervision* (Firth & Pajak, 1998) lists six references to coaching in the index, one of which is Cognitive Coaching, which is mentioned on six pages. All references are to coaching teachers.

Three sources were located that provide insight on

the impact of coaching principals. McDonough (1991) found that regardless of principals' training in Cognitive Coaching, they want similar things from their supervisors: increased capacity to be thoughtful, more effective instructional leaders, frequent interaction and collaboration, support that directly affects student success, a responsive relationship, a high level of trust, and support and understanding of their goals. These behaviors reflect the mission, concepts, and practices of Cognitive Coaching. McDonough concluded, "In general principals expressed a desire to learn from and modify themselves as a result of their experiences, to consider strategies from a variety of perspectives and to become increasingly flexible in their leadership strategies and supervisory behaviors" (p. 27).

Bradley (2006) provides strategies and guidance in the development of programs to mentor administrators to enhance their self-efficacy. She used the Delphi Technique, in which a panel of experts responded to five research questions in a series of four rounds. In each round the experts reached a facilitated consensus on the essential elements and barriers of effective mentoring for school site administrators. The process yielded seven key strategies: trust, confidentiality, time, process, belief in others, training, and communication. Evident in these strategies are the principles and practices of Cognitive Coaching. In fact, Bradley noted that "throughout the study the most predominant comprehensive mentoring methodology suggested by panel members was Cognitive Coaching."

Bloom, Castagna, Moir, and Warren (2005) describe a program of support for principals focused on coaching. However, the notion of blended strategies suggests a mixture rather than a mosaic of strategies designed to support the principal. The metaphor of a Möbius strip of coaching strategies results in a continuum that flows from instructional coaching to collaborative coaching to facilitative coaching. The coach is "able to fluidly draw upon a broad repertoire of strategies, including instructional strategies, in the course of any coaching conversation" (p. 57). In contrast, the focus of Cognitive Coaching is on self-directed learning by drawing on the internal resources of the person. The coach switches support functions (e.g., collaborator, consultant) in order to provide a different type of support and signals this switch so the principal knows which kind of support he or she is receiving. The coach offers strategies as a mosaic, something consisting of a number of things, rather than a blend that mixes different substances together so they do not readily separate.

Anticipated Outcomes

In the near absence of research on Cognitive Coaching of principals, the research on the outcomes of Cognitive Coaching with teachers holds promise of predicting the effect on principals. Table 3-1 lists eight outcomes of the research on Cognitive Coaching with teachers (Edwards, 2005), with our hypotheses on how these outcomes might relate to principals who receive Cognitive Coaching.

**Table 3-1. Comparison of Teacher Outcomes
With Anticipated Principal Outcomes**

Research-Based Outcomes With Teachers	Anticipated Outcomes With Principals
1. Cognitive Coaching was linked with increased student test scores and other benefits for students.	Principals who are coached will be more likely to coach teachers, which will result in increased student test scores and other benefits for students. Principals will be more focused as a result of Cognitive Coaching.

cont.

2. Teachers grew in teaching efficacy.	Principals will also grow in efficacy.
3. Cognitive Coaching impacted teachers' thinking, causing them to be more reflective and to think in more complex ways.	Principals' thinking will also be impacted, enabling them to be more reflective, as well as plan and problem-solve more effectively.
4. Teachers were more satisfied with their positions and with their choice of teaching as a profession.	Principals will also be more satisfied with their work, primarily as a result of feeling more resourceful and less stressed.
5. School cultures became more professional.	Principals will increase their ability to contribute to a more professional culture.
6. Teachers collaborated more.	Principals will collaborate more with their teachers, as well as with other building and central office administrators.
7. Cognitive Coaching assisted teachers professionally.	Cognitive Coaching will assist principals professionally by supporting them in becoming more reflective practitioners.
8. Cognitive Coaching benefited teachers personally.	Cognitive Coaching will benefit principals personally by decreasing stress levels.

In summary, we hypothesize that Cognitive Coaching will provide principals with a greater capacity for leadership as well as a form of job-embedded professional development. A review of the literature on using Cognitive

Coaching with principals revealed one study that indicated that when Cognitive Coaching became part of the weekly routine of principals, they became more thoughtful and reflective and felt more resourceful. Having a "sounding board" allowed principals time to think out loud about issues they might otherwise not have been able to discuss with others. This thinking led to more effective planning and decision making, as well as habituating of the behavior of thinking (Ellison & Hayes, 2003).

Two principals who received regular Cognitive Coaching from one of the authors of this book reflected at the end of the year on how coaching had supported them. One was a first-year principal who had been assigned midyear to a school in turmoil. She said that Cognitive Coaching support had saved her and her staff at least 2 years. In the year that she was coached, she felt that she was able to be more thoughtful and responsive in making decisions that kept the staff moving forward. Without the coaching, she said, she would have made many mistakes that would have resulted in slower progress toward building trust with her staff.

The other was a second-year principal who had received coaching as an assistant principal, but not in her first year as a principal. She said that the coaching made a difference in her emotional well-being. With coaching she wasn't as nervous about her interactions and decisions with the staff. Without coaching, she experienced more times when she was a "nervous wreck" about something happening at school. Coaching helped her not to second-guess herself and worry so much.

A Principal's Day

Imagine a principal sitting in his office thinking, and someone walking by saying, "What are you doing?" Would the principal reply, "I'm thinking"? Probably not, but it would be significant if he did. Saying so would be letting the teacher know that he values reflecting and engages in it on a regular basis. What different places our schools would be if we all took extended time to think each day. Schedules are so hectic and rushed that we're always moving on to the next thing. Planning is certainly part of a teacher's day, but what about reflecting? Wouldn't it be symbolic if, instead of having a planning period, teachers had a reflecting period?

Tables 3-2 and 3-3 show what one veteran elementary principal and one veteran secondary principal outlined as their activities on an average day. To a novice principal, these schedules probably appear to be an impossibility; however, they serve as a goal to which others might aspire. There is formal as well as informal time to meet with individual teachers, students, and parents; communicate with office staff; attend meetings; do paper work; respond to e-mail and phone calls; and, most important, to be in the classroom. The elementary principal even sets aside time in the day for reading! Notice what is missing, however. When do these principals have their thinking supported? When do they have an opportunity to have someone listen to and mediate their thinking?

Table 3-2. One Elementary Principal's Typical Day

Time	Activity
7:30	• Read and respond to e-mail and phone calls
8:00	• Informal interactions with staff • Scheduled meetings with staff • Tuesdays—team meetings • Thursdays—team leaders' meeting
9:00	• School begins—greet students and parents at front door

cont.

9:05	• Talk with office staff • Go through paperwork
9:15	• Literacy block—teach a group of students
10:15	• Formal and informal classroom observations
11:15	• Walk through cafeteria during each lunch period • Respond to e-mail and phone calls • Eat lunch with different teachers • Discipline students • Work on school improvement plan or other district work • Read
2:00	• Weekly leadership meeting • Classroom walk-throughs • Meet with teachers—pre- and post-observations • Meet with parents
3:50	• Dismissal—outside at buses • Informal interaction with parents and students
4:05	• Meetings with teachers—scheduled and informal • Answer phone calls and e-mail • Paper work • Site council or other meetings
5:00	• Leave school (later if after-school meeting runs longer or if there is an evening meeting)

Table 3-3. One Secondary Principal's Typical Day

Time	Activity
6:45	• Meet with office manager about day's calendar
7:00	• Walk around school for visibility • Meet with department chairpeople • Informal meetings with parents regarding problems
7:20	• Greet arriving students at front door
7:30	• Supervise students making announcements
7:40	• Scheduled meetings with parents • District meetings • Formal observations • Informal observations
11:30	• Supervise lunch • Walk around school • Meet with teachers
1:00	• Scheduled meetings with parents • District meetings • Formal observations • Informal observations
2:45	• Outside with buses for dismissal • Informal meetings with parents regarding problems
3:00	• Check on extracurricular activities • Attend committee meetings

cont.

5:00	• Leave unless evening responsibilities
7:00	• Sports, music programs, etc.—share attendance responsibilities with other administrators

An Action Research Project

One of the authors approached a school district, asking permission to conduct an action research project in which principals would receive weekly Cognitive Coaching. The hypothesis was that regular Cognitive Coaching would contribute to a feeling of greater resourcefulness and lower levels of stress. Sixteen building administrators volunteered to participate in the 4-month project. They scheduled meetings with a coach who came to their school once a week for 16 weeks and engaged in coaching conversations with them. Some of the comments of administrators at the end of the study were as follows:

- "Better focus on process and procedure; better forethought and reflection."
- "Time together helped me broaden my thinking for self-coaching."
- "I feel more confident in my current position."
- "Making time—30–45 minutes—for systematic reflecting and coaching allowed me to think and clarify situations, to explore options of action, and to plan steps."
- "These meetings have helped me determine my goals for the next 5 years."
- "As a first-year principal attempting to build a collaborative professional community, the coaching helped me to clarify my thinking around all issues, but especially around process and clear communication."

- "The weekly sessions enabled us to get to the heart of my leadership style versus a hit-and-miss problem format."

- "The reflection and planning I have done regarding my interactions with staff has increased. My listening to and accepting input from staff has increased."

- "Ultimately this means I am growing into a better leader, better planner, better principal."

The administrators who volunteered for the study constituted a diverse group, as shown in Table 3-4.

Table 3-4. Administrators Participating in the Action Research

Years of experience	1 to 14
Gender	14 men 2 women
Levels	15 elementary 1 middle
Positions	12 principals 4 assistant principals
Knowledge of Cognitive Coaching	10 Cognitive Coaching training 6 no training in Cognitive Coaching

One of the principals described the experience by saying, "It was total relaxation—my 'take me away, Calgon' moment." Most principals said they looked forward to the coaching session and often thought to themselves during the week, "That's something I want some coaching on." They would set that topic aside in their thinking until their coaching session and not worry, knowing that they were going to have time designated to focus on the topic. Some of the weekly sessions were a continuation of a previous week's conversation, whereas others focused on new content. The topic of conversation was the principal's or assistant principal's decision.

Following is a description of the process and assessment used in the action research project, as well as an analysis of the findings. The intention of this description is twofold: (a) provide a procedure for coaching principals in a district, and (b) provide data from one project to show how coaching supported principals. It is not necessary for others to replicate this process exactly; it is important to reflect on what might work in one's district.

Process

Time

The coach devoted 2 days a week to coaching the 16 administrators, scheduling to meet with 8 each day. Each administrator received a total of 6 to 8 hours of Cognitive Coaching over a period of 16 weeks. The number of sessions with each principal ranged from 10 to 13 sessions and lasted from 20 to 60 minutes; the average length of a session was 34 minutes. It was intentional that the sessions not be long, adding to an already tight schedule held by the administrators.

At each session, the administrator determined the content of the conversation. Based on what the administrator shared, the Cognitive Coaching conversation was structured around planning, reflecting and/or problem-resolving. The coach navigated within and among three of the support functions (coaching, collaborating, and consulting) to guide mediational interactions. The coach was an external consultant and not the evaluator of the administrators, so that support function was not engaged.

Journal

In addition to weekly coaching sessions, administrators responded to a weekly e-mail journal prompt. The intention of the journal was to enable the administrators to reflect on the effect the coaching had on their thinking and behavior, and to enable the researcher to establish content validity for the pre- and post-assessment that was used. The pre- and post-assessment instrument is described in the next section. The weekly journal prompt contained two questions: (a) How has the coaching session affected your thinking and perceptions? (b) How has the coaching session affected your behavior and actions?

Each week the journal entries were read independently by the co-directors of the Center for Cognitive Coaching to determine what States of Mind were present in the journals. The analysis of the journals indicated that the most frequently identified States of Mind were consciousness and craftsmanship. There was a .95 reliability between the co-directors when identifying consciousness, and a .75 reliability with craftsmanship. This finding was consistent with the informal assessment of the States of Mind made by the coach during conversations, as well as with the results of the self-assessment completed by each of the administrators. Here are two sample journal entries in response to the two questions mentioned above:

Entry 1

Wow! What a session. I thought it was a fantastic hour that altered my thinking profoundly. Our one conversation about how to present information to the G.T. teacher took an amazing turn. Instead of my presenting the information to the G.T. teacher, we present the information in a way that builds the interdependence of teachers and teams. What a wonderful way to help promote a learning organization! Also, our time spent in dialogue about a professional growth continuum will leave my brain working overtime. A long-term plan clearly defined with indicators would bring a much deeper purpose and meaning to the evaluation process. How to implement? Where to begin? Ouch, my head is hurting!

Actually, we have started planting the seeds already. Today in an "All About Kids!" meeting we were able to seize a moment and ask teachers about advanced kids and how they are seeing the support from the G.T. teachers. However, we did not form agreements or talk about specific numbers…our next step.

Thanks for your time. I'm sure after 15 or so sessions each week, topics must be a little repetitive…but I always feel you are right there with me. Thanks for helping me dig deeper!

Entry 2

This process, not just yesterday's conversation, has helped me to focus on my leadership style. As we talk, I realize that my natural style is very effective with four of the six teams. Yesterday's conversation helped me to focus on the best approach to my work with my first and fifth.

Our conversations have helped me to differentiate my leadership style for these two teams. I am finding that I am much more direct with both first and fifth. I made up my mind before meeting with the first grade this week that the recess issue was not up for discussion but I knew that if I just walked in and gave that directive without data, it would not have worked. My natural inclination is to think through a problem. I rarely leap without looking. This trait allowed me to wait for the data necessary to support my request. Our conversations on the importance of data made this work.

Switching Support Functions

At times the coach made an intentional decision to step out of coaching to consult or collaborate with the administrator (see chapter 4). In the 181 coaching sessions in the project, the coach switched to consulting 97 times and to collaborating 3 times. Collaborating took the form of co-brainstorming. In two cases, it was to brainstorm ideas for supporting a teacher who was struggling; in one case it was to develop an agenda for a staff meeting. Consulting most often took the form of providing a menu of options, thinking aloud, role-playing, or referencing current research. The topics on which the coach most often consulted were Cognitive Coaching tools (e.g., paraphrasing, rapport) and content from the Adaptive Schools work (e.g., decision-making process) (Garmston & Wellman, 2000). The total amount of time spent in consulting ranged from 4 to 31 minutes. The principal who received a total of 8 hours of coaching was in his first year as a principal; he was also the principal who received 31 minutes of consulting. That means that 94% of the time was spent in Cognitive Coaching.

> The decision to switch from the support function of Cognitive Coaching was made when the administrator's resources were not evident.

The decision to switch from the support function of Cognitive Coaching was made when the administrator's resources were not evident. This determination was made after beginning the conversation with Cognitive Coaching. Doing so allowed the coach to determine three things: (a) what other support function might better support thinking, (b) what might be said as the consultant or collaborator, and (c) what consulting or collaborating strategy was most appropriate. In such cases, the coach signaled the switch—first by asking for permission from the administrator (e.g., "Would you like some options to consider?" or "Would you like to brainstorm some ideas?"). and second by disengaging rapport. In each case the coach was able to return to the support function of Cognitive Coaching and ask a question that would allow the administrator to engage with the content (e.g., "So what do you think might work for you?" or "What meaning do you make from that?"). The intent of the coach was always to support self-directed learning, even when consulting or collaborating.

Assessment

Pre- and Post-Assessment States of Mind Surveys

Participants completed a pre- and post-assessment of their resourcefulness in the five States of Mind: consciousness, craftsmanship, efficacy, flexibility, and interdependence. The instrument was adapted from one developed by the co-directors for the Center for Cognitive Coaching in 1998, to support teams in diagnosing groups' States of Mind. Forty items that included eight statements about each State of Mind composed the survey. Following are some items from the survey, each one focusing on a different State of Mind:

- I usually consider several ways of doing something before deciding what might work best.
- My communication with others rarely needs clarifying.
- I feel like I make a difference in this district.
- On most days, I take time to reflect on my work.
- I feel valued by staff members.

For each item, a point value was assigned to the response: 4 = Strongly Agree, 3 = Agree, 2 = Disagree, 1 = Strongly Disagree. The responses for each item were totaled, and an average determined for each State of Mind. The ratings from the pre-assessment were compared with the ratings from the post-assessment, and an increase or decrease was determined. Table 3-5 shows the difference in the administrators' pre- and post-assessments.

Table 3-5. Administrators' Pre- and Post-Assessment Difference

Adm.	Efficacy	Conscious-ness	Crafts-man-ship	Flexi-bility	Inter-depend-ence
1	+1.5	+4	+1.5	+3	+1
2	−1	−2	+2	+1	+2
3	−2	+2	+4	+1	+2
4	+5	+10	+1	+7	+2
5	−1	+1	0	−3	−2
6	+5.5	+5	+5.5	+4	+3.5
7		INCOMPLETE	DATA		
8	−1	+1	+1	+2	−2
9	+1	+5	−5	+7	+4
10	+6	+6	+4	+1	+3
11	0	+4.5	+5.5	+3	+5.5
12	−1	0	+1	+3	+3
13	+3	+1	+5	+3	+5
14	+6	+6	+1	+6	+4
15	+1	+1	+2	0	−1
16	+1	+4.5	+2	+2	+3.5

Four administrators perceived their resourcefulness as having decreased in one State of Mind, two administrators decreased in two States of Mind, and one administrator rated his resourcefulness as decreasing in three States of Mind. Three administrators perceived that their resourcefulness had remained unchanged in one State of Mind. Two administrators had incomplete data.

To triangulate the data, administrators asked three staff members to complete the survey. They agreed that the three staff members would be their office manager, one teacher who was supportive of the principal, and one teacher who was not supportive. The intention was to gather data from a variety of perspectives. The ratings of the three staff members were then averaged. Table A-1 in the Appendix shows the difference in the average of the three staff members' pre- and post-assessments as increases or decreases. The results indicated that half the participants showed increases in all States of Mind as perceived by their staffs. Of the half that showed decreases as perceived by their staff members, three administrators decreased in one State of Mind, one decreased in two States of Mind, two decreased in four States of Mind and two decreased in all five States of Mind. One administrator had incomplete data.

The administrators' supervisor also completed the pre- and post- assessment. Table A-2 in the Appendix shows the differences in the supervisors' pre- and post-assessments. Four administrators were perceived by their supervisors as having lowered resourcefulness in one or more States of Mind; of the four, two administrators decreased in two States of Mind and two administrators decreased in three States of Mind. Nine received increases in all five States of Mind, including some of the greatest increases in the study.

Table A-3 in the Appendix shows the comparison of the three sources of data for each administrator. The first row is the self-assessment, the second is the staff's perceptions, and the third row is the supervisor's perceptions. The decreased ratings are summarized here in Table 3-6 for each administrator.

**Table 3-6. Sources of Decreased Resourcefulness
in the Five States of Mind**

No.	Efficacy	Con-scious-ness	Crafts-man-ship	Flex-ibility	Inter-depend-ence
1					staff
2	self	self	staff	staff	
3	self				
4				super-visor	
5	self & staff		staff	self & staff	self & staff
6		staff			
7					
8	self & staff	staff & super-visor	staff & super-visor	staff & super-visor	self & staff
9			self		
10					
11					
12	self		super-visor	super-visor	
13		super-visor	super-visor	super-visor	
14					
15	staff	staff	staff	staff	self
16	staff	staff	staff	staff	staff

A review of the comparisons of data from the three sources reveals some key findings. Four administrators received increases in all States of Mind, and five received a decrease in only one State of Mind from one of the sources. For those nine administrators, there was a consistency in the perceptions from the three sources. Of the remaining seven, three received decreases from a combination of self and staff, one received decreases from a combination of self and supervisor, one from supervisor only, one from staff only, and one from a combination of self, staff, and supervisor. The source of the majority of the decreases is staff. It is important to keep in mind that the three staff members comprised the office manager, a staff member supportive of the principal, and a staff member who was not supportive of the principal.

Because some of the administrators participating in the study were familiar with Cognitive Coaching and some were not, the researcher asked each administrator to complete the pre-assessment a second time, at the end of the study. It was hypothesized that the project enabled them to have a more informed view of their States of Mind. Table A-4 in the Appendix shows the comparison of the post-assessment with the second administration of the pre-assessment (the "post-pre-"). In this comparison, only three administrators had a decreased resourcefulness in any State of Mind, compared to seven in the original pre-assessment. One explanation for the difference in perceptions is that as a result of participating in the study, the administrators gained a greater understanding of the five States of Mind. With this increased understanding, they could more accurately assess their resources in the five States of Mind at the beginning of the study.

Final Survey

A final written survey was administered after the last coaching session. The respondents could answer *not at all*, *somewhat*, or *very much*, and add comments to the following questions:

1. How important was it that your Cognitive Coach was not your supervisor?

2. How important was it that your Cognitive Coach had experience as an elementary principal?

3. To what extent do you trust your Cognitive Coach? If somewhat or very much, what is the basis for your trust of your Cognitive Coach?

4. How has ongoing, weekly coaching supported your professional and personal capacities as a principal?

5. What other comments do you have?

The results of the final survey revealed that (a) trust was important to all participants; (b) all but one participant felt it was important that their Cognitive Coach was not their supervisor; (c) the coach's experience as an elementary principal was valuable to all participants. The survey data suggested that administrators preferred a coach who was not their evaluator. Building trust and decreasing the principal's sense of vulnerability were important because they allowed the principal to get at the heart of issues without fear of negative consequences. These findings are addressed in chapter 4 as a key in deciding who should provide Cognitive Coaching support to principals.

Analysis of the Data

The Most Important Point

One point that stands out is the predominance of the increases in ratings. Even the ratings that are decreased are smaller in value than most of the increased ratings. However, it would not be accurate to use numbers alone to determine the increased resourcefulness of the administrators. Responding *strongly agree* to every item on the survey would yield a rating of 32 in each State of Mind. A participant who was rated high by the staff or supervisor before the survey might have a lower increase than one who was rated lower before the survey. Another example of the numbers not telling the whole story is that there were some 1s (*strongly disagree*) given on the pre-survey, but no one was assigned a 1 on the post-survey. All one can say as a result of looking at the numbers is that most of the principals thought they had, and were perceived as having, increased resources, as measured by the survey, at the end of the study.

The Most Significant Data

Given the hypothesis of the study, perhaps the most significant data comes from the self-assessment. If participants felt more resourceful, that in itself would contribute toward a lower level of stress. Table 3-5 indicates that six participants (nos. 3, 8, 9, 12, and 15) showed slightly lower scores in one or two States of Mind; one participant (no. 5) was lower in three States of Mind. However, the "post-pre-" scores in Table A-4 reveal that all the differences are positive, with the exception of two (nos. 9 and 12).

There does not seem to be a correlation between administrators' "post-pre-" scores and attendance at the Cognitive Coaching foundation Seminar. That is, those who attended the seminar (nos. 1, 2, 4, 7, 8, 9, 10, 13, 15, and 16) did not seem to have post-pre-assessments that were more closely aligned with their post-assessments. One way to account for this is that the administrators did not maintain the awareness of their Cognitive Coaching skills or States of Mind since attending the training. One administrator even remarked that as a result of being coached, she was coaching her staff more. The process of being coached reminded her of the power of coaching.

Probably the second most important set of data is the supervisor's assessment of the administrator's resourcefulness (Table A-2). If a supervisor believes that an administrator is, and treats an administrator as, more resourceful, that might contribute to lower stress on the part of the administrator. This category of data contained the least number of decreased ratings, with four administrators (nos. 4,

8, 12, and 13). Two had decreased ratings in two States of Mind (nos. 4 and 12) and two had decreased ratings in three States of Mind (nos. 8 and 13). Efficacy stands out as the only State of Mind without a decreased rating. This finding is consistent with the research on the outcomes of using Cognitive Coaching with teachers.

The Interrelationship of the Data

If we compare the decreased self-assessment ratings with the decreased supervisor ratings in Table 3-6, we see that two administrators fell into both groups (nos. 8 and 12). Their self-perception and the perception of their supervisors was that there was lowered resourcefulness in some States of Mind. With administrator number 8, there is some consistency in the States of Mind that decreased; in administrator number 12, there does not seem to be a correlation between the decreased ratings (Table A-3). Using the data alone, it is difficult to explain this result.

The pre- and post-assessment ratings of the staff (Table A-1) were an average of the three staff members who completed the survey about the administrator. Eight administrators (nos. 1, 2, 5, 6, 8, 14, 15, and 16) had decreased ratings in one or more States of Mind, as surveyed by their staff. Of those eight, three (nos. 2, 5, and 15) had decreased ratings from their self-assessment, and one (no. 8) had decreased ratings from all three assessers (Table A-3).

Earlier it was suggested that the numbers do not tell the whole story, and two sets of data from the staff support that assumption. The two administrators who were rated lower by their staff at the end of the study in all five States of Mind (nos. 8 and 16) had scores that looked very different. The range on number 16's average ratings was from 30 to 32; the range on number 8's was from 21.5 to 28. The decreased ratings of number 8 might also be attributed to the fact that only two of the three staff members completed the post-assessment, and one of the three pre-assessments contained almost all 4s (*strongly agree*). On the other hand, administrator number 16 had little room for improvement, because the pre-assessment average was 30.

Five of the administrators (nos. 1, 7, 10, 12, and 13) asked their supervisor if they could continue with the coaching after the 4-month period ended. As a result of that request, they received 13 additional weeks of Cognitive Coaching. None of them had any decreased ratings from their staff's assessments; one (no. 12) had a decreased rating in the self-assessment, and two (nos. 12 and 13) had decreased ratings from their supervisors. This might suggest that it is the quality, not the quantity, of coaching that is important. This aspect of quality over quantity is significant, given that the principal's day is very busy. Coaching does not have to take a great deal of time out of the principal's day, because it is the quality of the coaching that is key in determining the effectiveness of the process. Coaching that moves below the surface to the deep structure of a person's beliefs, values, goals, mental models, and identity is more effective than coaching that remains on the surface. A short amount of time with a highly qualified coach is more beneficial than a longer time with a coach who is not well trained for the job.

Patterns and Trends

One pattern is the increased resourcefulness of administrators from the beginning of the study to the end. In the self-assessment data (Table 3-5), there is a pattern with the States of Mind. Efficacy initially had more decreases in ratings (nos. 2, 3, 5, 8, and 12) than any other State of Mind; however, in the "post-pre-" assessment (Table A-4) there is only one decrease in efficacy from the beginning of the study to the end (no. 12). Consciousness, craftsmanship, and flexibility each had one decrease (nos. 2, 9, and 5, respectively), and interdependence had three decreased ratings (nos. 5, 8, and 15), but in the "post-pre-" there was only one decrease in craftsmanship (no. 9) and one in interdependence (no. 4). It would appear that participating in

> *It would appear that participating in the study gave administrators a clearer understanding of their States of Mind.*

the study gave administrators a clearer understanding of their States of Mind.

Another pattern is in the self-assessment data (Table 3-5) from the assistant principals (nos. 11, 13, 15, and 16). Some of the greatest increases occurred for these administrators. At some time during the study, each of them indicated that the coaching was the most valuable professional experience in which they had engaged. During the course of the study one assistant was appointed as a principal. Within 2 years of the completion of the study, all the assistants who participated became principals. Although this statistic is significant, one cannot conclude that the coaching was the key variable. The fact that they volunteered for the project says a great deal about their professional growth goals.

It is important to recognize that all the administrators in this study volunteered to participate. Their verbal comments—along with the data from the surveys, most profoundly from their self-assessment—indicate that weekly Cognitive Coaching did make a difference in their resourcefulness. In addition to the nonjudgmental coaching, the regularity of the scheduled support made Cognitive Coaching different from other kinds of mentoring they had received. One assistant principal remarked that the coaching sessions were more like a long conversation that she could continue each week, picking up the threads from the previous week.

This study indicates that building administrators do increase in resourcefulness in the five States of Mind when they receive regular Cognitive Coaching. The implication is that districts should be mobilizing resources to determine how they can provide Cognitive Coaching to principals and assistant principals on a regular basis. Building administrators want, need, and deserve the same support they are striving to provide for their staffs. The investment a district makes in supporting principals with Cognitive Coaching will pay dividends in the future.

The Need for More Research

Clearly, there is a need for more research on coaching principals. Given the research on coaching teachers, one would anticipate that many of the outcomes of coaching principals would mirror the outcomes of coaching teachers. Among other things, principals would be more resourceful leaders and more satisfied with their jobs. Under those conditions they would be more likely to stay in their positions, thus providing consistency and continuity of leadership in the district. Perhaps the principalship will become a more attractive option for educators. Today's emphasis on data in education calls for scientifically based research to show that coaching principals results in more effective teaching and learning in our schools.

References

Bloom, G., Castagna, C., Moir, E., & Warren, B. (2005). *Blended coaching: Skills and strategies to support principal development*. Thousand Oaks, CA: Corwin Press.

Bradley, A. (2006). *Study of implementation barriers and strategies for success of effective mentoring for school administrators*. Ph.D. dissertation University of LaVerne, LaVerne, CA.

Edwards, J. (2005). *Cognitive Coaching research*. Center for Cognitive Coaching. Available online at www.cognitivecoaching.com.

Ellison, J., & Hayes, C. (2003) *Cognitive Coaching: Weaving threads of learning and change into the culture of an organization*. Norwood, MA: Christopher-Gordon.

Firth, G., & Pajak, E. (1998). *Handbook of research on school supervision*. New York: Simon & Schuster Macmillan.

Garmston, R., & Wellman, B. (2000). *Adaptive schools: Facilitating collaborative groups.* Norwood, MA: Christopher-Gordon.

McDonough, S. (1991). *The supervision of principals: A comparison of existing and desired supervisory practices as perceived by principals trained in Cognitive Coaching and those without the training.* Unpublished master's thesis, University of California, Sacramento.

4

Who Should Provide Cognitive Coaching to Principals?

The question of who should provide Cognitive Coaching to principals has different answers, depending on the district's personnel, finances, culture, and history of principal supervision. Personnel is a major consideration, because many districts might not have enough staff to be able to allocate the responsibility for coaching principals to designated individuals. Finances can determine the form of the coaching; whether someone is hired from outside the district to coach principals or someone internally has the responsibility added to their current position will result in different costs. Also included in the financial considerations should be the cost of losing a principal after only a few years of service. The district's culture can affect the decision as it relates to the customary relationship between principals and their supervisors. Cognitive Coaching would be a misfit in a district in which principals are reinforced for "keeping the lid on" at their schools. Cognitive Coaching is more congruent in a culture that supports thinking and collaborating among staff. Finally, related to culture is the district's history of principal supervision. How principals have been supervised in the past is probably the way in which principals anticipate being supervised in the future.

In this chapter, a variety of factors will be considered to support districts in coming to their own conclusions about who should provide the support. Regardless of personnel, finances, culture, and history, three factors are important to consider in selecting the principal's coach in order to ensure a successful program of support: trust, confidentiality, and training.

Trust

Fundamental to the success of any coaching program is trust between the coach and coachee. The importance of trust in schools is well documented (Bryk & Schneider, 2001; Tschannen-Moran, 2004), and the role of the principal in establishing and maintaining trust is essential. If a climate of trust is the principal's responsibility, then trust between a principal and a coach is equally important. In the principal-coach relationship, two concepts about trust are critical: (a) In situations of high trust, people do not hesitate to seek help, because they do not fear that others will think they are inadequate; (b) without the confidence that a person's words can be relied upon and can accurately describe future actions, trust is unlikely to develop.

Without trust, the principal might fear that the coach will perceive him as inadequate, and therefore he will not be as forthcoming about his thoughts and actions. This is even more important with a veteran principal, who might think that she is expected to know things she does not. A novice principal might be more willing to admit that he does not know something, but he also has the pressure to prove himself as competent and capable. Cognitive Coaching support holds potential benefits for both novice and veteran, but if the principal does not feel safe being open and honest in communicating with the coach, the coaching will probably not be effective, regardless of the principal's level of experience.

To be trustworthy, one must be viewed as someone who tells the truth and keeps one's word. If the principal does not feel sure that she can rely upon the coach's word, she will not see the coach as providing much help. If the coach tells the principal that he will do something, the principal needs to feel that she can rely on the coach to do what he says he will. For example, if the coach tells the principal that their conversations are confidential, and the principal finds out later that the coach has talked with someone about their conversation, then the principal will have a difficult time believing that she can trust the coach in the future. In such cases of broken trust, the coach would have to work hard to regain the trust of the principal. Keeping one's word also means remembering appointments, being on time, and following through with commitments. From the standpoint of developing trust, it is better not to make a commitment than to make one that cannot be fulfilled.

The research on trust in schools offers insight into the development of trust between a principal and a coach. Megan Tschannen-Moran (2004) concludes that there are five facets that people rely on in making trust judgments: benevolence, honesty, openness, reliability, and competence. Table 4-1 summarizes the key aspects of each facet.

Table 4-1. Facets of Trust

Benevolence	Caring, extending good will, having positive intentions, supporting teachers, expressing appreciation for staff efforts, being fair, guarding confidential information
Honesty	Having integrity, telling the truth, keeping promises, honoring agreements, having authenticity, accepting responsibility, avoiding manipulation, being real, being true to oneself

cont.

Openness	Engaging in open communication, sharing important information, delegating, sharing decision making, sharing power
Reliability	Having consistency, being dependable, demonstrating commitment, having dedication, being diligent
Competence	Setting an example, engaging in problem solving, fostering conflict resolution, working hard, pressing for results, setting standards, buffering teachers, handling difficult situations, being flexible

Other research indicates that staffs trust a principal who demonstrates competence, consistency, evenhanded behavior and integrity (Bryk & Schneider, 2001). Competence is defined by Tschannen-Moran (2004) as "the ability to perform a task as expected, according to appropriate standards." When one is new to a position, it is sometimes difficult for others to gauge one's competence. In such cases, one's reputation plays a key role in the establishment of trust. If a person is preceded by a reputation of competence, it provides a jump start to building a trusting relationship. One principal expressed this about her coach by saying, "Her reputation as a coach, as relayed from my colleague, reinforced my trust." Another principal said, "Her reputation and previous experience with her never presented any concerns about trust." Similarly, a negative reputation can cause difficulty in the establishment of trust.

It is quite interesting, however, that research indicates that competence is not a factor in determining trust between teachers (Tschannen-Moran, 2004). The main factors here are benevolence (e.g., covering a class or taking food to someone's home), honesty, and openness (e.g., sharing knowledge and skills). Nevertheless, Tschannen-Moran speculates that the current emphasis on accountability and shared decision making is rapidly leading to competence becoming a factor in teacher-to-teacher trust. For example, third-grade teachers (whose students take a statewide test for the first time) will tell you that the competence of the kindergarten through second-grade teachers matters a great deal to them.

Consistency and evenhanded behavior go together. A consistent person is predictable; others can anticipate what the person might do or say in a given situation. One can be human and have ups and downs, but over time there is a consistent pattern to one's behavior. An inconsistent person is someone you have to check out with a third party before approaching him or her. For example, you might ask someone else, "Is this a good day to talk to X about my concerns about our team?" An inconsistent principal gives different answers to the same question depending on who is asking. A consistent, evenhanded principal is someone whose behavior others can anticipate and predict. Staff members can say with confidence, "Our principal is always there for us," or "Our principal would never do that to us."

Integrity is defined as telling the truth, keeping promises, and being authentic (Tschannen-Moran & Hoy, 2000). A way of explaining authenticity is to say that the principal is a person first and the role second. For example, let's say that a principal arrives at school and hears through the grapevine that a teacher was up all night with a sick child. It so happens that the principal has an observation scheduled with the teacher that day. A principal who leads with the role will go to the teacher and say, "I know you must be exhausted, but you know how hard it is for me to get all my observations done; I'll be in your room as scheduled at nine o'clock." The authentic principal would say, "I know you must be exhausted. Would you like to reschedule your observation?" That principal relates to the teacher as a person first, understanding how the teacher must feel and relating in a caring and empathetic way.

Research also cites five leadership behaviors that cultivate trust: consistency, integrity, concern, communication, and sharing control (Tschannen-Moran & Hoy, 2000). A concerned leader cares about the employees beyond their life at work, engaging them in conversations about family, interests, and hobbies. The teacher of a concerned principal is a professional friend and not just an employee.

Communication is essential in any organization, and a leader's ability to communicate clearly, concisely, openly, and honestly is critical to the development of trust. With the advent of technology in schools comes an increased awareness of the importance of face-to-face communication. Many agree that if a topic is potentially sensitive, it should be addressed in person rather than left to the uncertain interpretations that can result from e-mails.

Sharing control involves shared decision making. Trustworthy leaders share control by being clear about the decision-making process and ensuring that those affected by a decision have a say in the outcome. Sharing control does not mean that the principal turns over most of the decisions to others. A principal who shares control knows, or is advised by a leadership council, which decisions should be made by the principal, which should be made by the council, and which should be made by the staff. Sharing control is essential in the hiring of staff. Principals often believe that this means allowing staff members to make the decision of who should be hired. Actually, the principal should make this decision with input from staff members. Allowing the staff to make such a decision is not only harmful to collaboration, it is also potentially uncomfortable for staff. If the newly hired staff member has difficulties on the job, it is the principal, not the staff members, who will have to intervene. In a collaborative culture, the principal usually follows the recommendation of staff members for hiring; if the principal does not, it is important for him or her to explain why. Sharing control means being clear about and understanding who has control when and why.

Costa and Garmston (2002), the co-developers of Cognitive Coaching, identify four themes in the trust literature: trust in oneself, trust between individuals, trust in the coaching relationship, and trust in the environment. They see trust in oneself as a prerequisite for any trusting relationship with others, and believe that it is important for coaches to be conscious and clear about their own values and beliefs. Trust between individuals is influenced by each person's image of trust and perception of trustworthiness of the other person. Clear goals, roles, and expectations define trust in the coaching relationship. Trust in the environment is critical because it signals the degree to which people in that environment trust each other. For example, if a person works in an environment where right answers are more valued than reflective thought, it would be difficult for the person to engage in a process like Cognitive Coaching. "The effective coach also works to create, monitor, and maintain a stimulating, mediational, and cooperative environment deliberately designed to sustain and enhance trust" (p. 204).

Bryk and Schneider (2001) found five criteria for the discernment of trust: respect, competence, personal regard for others, and integrity. These are lenses that we look through to determine whether or not we will trust another person and through which others look at us. With the exception of respect, all the criteria have been noted in other research. Respect involves two aspects: (a) the extent to which one's role with students is viewed as important, and (b) the degree to which one can depend on others involved. Respect is created through the conversations that take place in schools and the genuine listening that indicates that attention is being given to what a person says.

In summary, the research on trust in schools has a direct application to the relationship of the coach and the principal. In order to establish a trusting relationship, the principal needs to view the coach as benevolent, honest, open, reliable, competent, consistent, concerned, and authentic. In turn the coach needs to trust himself, the principal, the relationship, and the environment. It is unusual that we trust someone upon meeting them for the first time, but beginning a relationship that develops with these qualities will, over time, result in trust. As one principal said of her coach, "She offered me objective coaching and clarified my thinking so effectively in the first couple of sessions that trust and rapport were fairly immediate."

Confidentiality

> *A successful coaching relationship is based on the same premise as attorney-client privilege or the doctor-patient relationship.*

Trust and confidentiality support each other. It is often easy to say that the coach and the principal have a confidential relationship, but sometimes that confidence is difficult to maintain. A successful coaching relationship is based on the same premise as attorney-client privilege or the doctor-patient relationship.

Unless the principal discloses behavior that is illegal or immoral, the coach should not discuss it with anyone. In the rare cases where such a disclosure is made, the coach should encourage the principal to talk with the supervisor. If the principal chooses not to do that, the coach will have to tell the principal that she will talk with the supervisor.

More typical of the challenge of maintaining confidentiality is the awareness of this when the coach is talking with friends or acquaintances. A principal has the right to expect that the coach will keep the content of their conversations out of discussions with others, and the coach has the responsibility to maintain confidential information as private.

Confidentiality is critical to two of the aspects of trust:

openness and honesty. In order to have an effective coaching relationship, the principal must know that what he or she says to a coach will not be repeated (without permission). In one instance a person whose friend was a staff member at the same school was coaching the principal of the school. When the principal gave the coach's friend a negative evaluation, the coach was careful, when talking to the principal, not to mention anything the friend had said, and when talking to the friend, not to mention anything the principal had said. The coach knew that she had maintained the confidence of both parties even as both continued to talk to her about the process.

Although the tools of a Cognitive Coach are similar to those used in therapeutic settings, it is imperative that a coach know the difference. A therapist's job is to break down defenses, to take the person where he or she might not want to go. A Cognitive Coach's job is to take the person where he or she *wants* to go. Think of a person as having various layers of the self. The outer layer is information you will volunteer (e.g., your name, where you're from, your job); the next layer is information you will provide if asked (e.g., how long you've had your job, where you went to school, where you grew up), but don't ordinarily share unless asked. The third layer is information that is intimate, that you share only with close friends. The fourth layer is your private self, that you share only with a significant other or keep to yourself. The fifth layer is the unknown self, the things about yourself of which you are not even conscious. The three inner layers are the territory of therapy. Cognitive Coaching focuses on the outer two layers (Ellison & Hayes, 2005). Sometimes a person reveals the third layer (information that is intimate) in a coaching conversation; when this happens, the coach must be highly conscious of the nature of the information in order to determine if it should remain part of a coaching conversation or if the person needs professional therapy.

Following is a conversation in which intimate information was appropriately revealed in a Cognitive Coaching situation:

P: I'm exhausted just looking at my calendar. I don't know how I'm going to get everything done. I thought that after a couple of years, I would get the hang of it all and be able to be more flexible with my time, but now it seems I busier than ever.

C: So you're overwhelmed with all the work you have to do and disappointed in yourself for not getting more control after 2 years.

P: Yes! I want to have more time for my family. My kids are in high school and middle school, and I like attending their activities and spending time with them when they're home. And my husband and I like to travel.

C: So even though you are a very busy person, it's important to you that your work not consume your life.

P: Exactly! You hit the nail on the head!

C: So when do remember your life not being so busy?

P: Well, not when I was teaching—I was always busy, I never sat still. I was planning lessons, teaching, working on committees, meeting with parents, going to workshops. There was never enough time to get everything done.

C: So you have had the identity as a busy person for a long time.

P: Yes, I have! When I think back I guess it started when I was a kid [*long pause*]. My mother never let us say that we were bored. We always had to be doing something. Oh, My gosh! [*Long pause and tears*] I'm busy today because I learned to stay busy when I was a kid!

The principal's sharing of intimate information is appropriate within the context of a coaching conversation. Realizing that she had always been busy, even as a child, helped her to understand why her calendar seemed to be out of control. Her increased consciousness resulted in a breakthrough in her thinking. Although it surfaced childhood experiences, there was no trauma involved with the memories.

In the next scenario, the coach handles the sharing of intimate information by an assistant principal (AP) in a different way:

C: So, how are things going?

AP: Well, not so good. I'm not feeling comfortable with my principal, and as her assistant I'm supposed to be supporting her. But she and I are not at all alike, and I can never figure out what she wants me to do.

C: You're unsure as to how to relate to your principal in a way that supports the work of your school.

AP: That's right. This is really different from being in a classroom. When I was in the classroom, I spent most of the day with kids on my own. But now as an assistant principal I'm constantly dealing with problems the staff brings to me. The student discipline issues are not a problem, but I don't always know how I'm supposed to respond to the teachers. Many of them are her friends, and, frankly, I think my principal and some of the teachers don't like me. Sometimes I think she sets me up to not look so good.

C: So you're not feeling supported and therefore are not being supportive.

AP: Right! You know, I went through a messy divorce a few years back, and I don't need negativity in my life. I paid for a lot of therapy to learn who I am and how to feel good about myself. Sometimes my principal makes me feel the same way my ex-wife did.

C: So your professional relationship with your principal is causing you to relive some of the pain of your divorce.

AP: Yeah, I guess it is.

C: When did you stop the therapy?

AP: I quit about a year ago. I thought I had resolved everything and was feeling pretty good, until now.

C: Given what you're going through with your principal, I would recommend that you consider returning to therapy. I'm not qualified to help you with these issues.

AP: Thanks. Maybe I'll do that. If I get therapy, can you still coach me around some of the work issues?

C: Sure, I'd be glad to coach you on work-related topics. I'm glad you see the need for both coaching and therapeutic support.

In this scenario, when the assistant principal shared intimate information about his divorce, the coach realized that she was not qualified to support him and suggested therapy. It is important that the person being coached not feel judged by the coach. The trust that is built between the coach and the principal should enable a positive outcome in such situations.

Another aspect of confidentiality involves communication between the coach and the principal's supervisor. In the most effective coaching relationships, the coach does not have input in the evaluation process. One district refers to a "data curtain" that prevents the coach from communicating information from coaching sessions to the principal's evaluator. The coach does not volunteer information, nor does the supervisor request information about the principal. The effectiveness of the coaching should be judged by the outcome, not by what happens during coaching conversations.

Training

The value and importance of training a coach cannot be overestimated. The training determines the coach's competence, which in turn is a factor in establishing trust. Moreover, without training, a coach follows his or her intuition, which, though possibly effective, has two limitations. Because intuitive behavior is unconscious, it cannot be called upon when needed, and it cannot be taught or explained to another person. A successful coach has a repertoire of skills and strategies, like a tool kit, from which he or she selects the most appropriate ones at any given time. If this tool kit is unconscious, the coach has a limited capacity to support a principal.

We believe in Cognitive Coaching as the primary resource in training coaches to support principals (see chapter 2). The co-developers of Cognitive Coaching, Arthur Costa and Robert Garmston, created the model in 1984 as a process for principals to use to support the thinking of teachers. Since then Cognitive Coaching has been applied in teacher-teacher, teacher-student, and teacher-parent relationships. Because the principles and practices of Cognitive Coaching support the development of self-directedness in others, it is perfect as a means of supporting principals. With training, the Cognitive Coach is a neutral, nonjudgmental listener who draws on the internal resources of the principal and builds the capacity of the principal to plan, reflect, and problem-solve on his or her own.

The 8-day Cognitive Coaching Foundation® seminar is based on constructivist learning theory and provides many opportunities for practice. Although there is a great deal of declarative knowledge in Cognitive Coaching (e.g., States of Mind, holonomy, self-directedness), the maps and tools used by a coach are procedural knowledge. In order to be internalized, procedural knowledge must be practiced. The training includes an initial practice of every concept introduced, with the expectation that participants will learn even more from their practice outside the training.

The training is divided into two parts of 4 days each. In part 1, participants learn ways to expand and refine their knowledge and skills to support the thinking of others, thereby affecting behavior and ultimately enhancing performance. The focus is on strategies that enhance intellectual growth and strengthen decision making. Part 1 includes the learning of two conversation structures (planning and reflecting) and four communication tools (pausing, paraphrasing, probing, inquiring). Specifically, participants learn to establish rapport and create trust, facilitate learning through structured conversations, develop teacher self-confidence and cognitive autonomy, and develop a sense of community within a school.

In part 2, participants learn a third conversation structure (problem-resolving) and two tool clusters (pacing and leading). Specifically, participants learn to recognize when a person has had a breakthrough in thinking, help others when they are stuck in their thinking, and apply a repertoire of strategies for mediating another person's thinking.

Selecting Someone to Coach Principals

Generally, the arrangement for coaching is made between the principal and the person he or she has selected as a coach. Sometimes a supervisor requests coaching for the principal; then it is important that the principal agrees with the process and wants to be coached. If coaching is an intervention that the principal does not want, the process will probably fail. In order for there to be an effective coaching relationship, both parties must be willing participants.

Internal or External

The coach may be a person employed by the district or an independent consultant with whom the district contracts. Regardless of whether the coach is a person within the district or someone contracted from outside the district, trust, confidentiality, and training are essential. An in-district coach is often a "known quantity" to others in the district. If he is not regarded as a trustworthy and confidential person by those who know him, regardless of the training he receives, the likelihood of having successful coaching relationships is small. On the other hand, selecting a district person who is respected and trusted will result in a shorter amount of time required to establish trust. An out-of-district person whose positive reputation is known to principals will experience the same benefits in establishing trust. If the coach is a person hired outside the district and is not known to the principals, she can expect to spend more time developing trust.

For a coach who is known to principals, trust and confidentiality are prerequisites for the training. That is, if the person is known to be untrustworthy, the training probably won't matter. If the person is not known to principals, the training will allow him or her to demonstrate competence as well as establish trust and maintain confidentiality.

One of the main challenges in having an internal coach is adding to the already busy schedule of a district employee. Ideally, if the district selects an internal person to coach principals, coaching should be a full-time job. To have the relationships necessary to coach principals, the coach needs to have frequent, even if short, contact with each principal. The action research project described in chapter 4 indicated that the average time the coach spent with a principal was 34 minutes a week; it is important that the coaching sessions do not add to an already overwhelming schedule that most principals maintain. A coach who does not see a principal for a long period of time will not be as attuned to what is going on in that principal's life and will need to spend more time catching up on his or her thinking. Our experience has been that frequency, how often a coach sees a principal, is more important than duration, how long each session is. Of course, both frequency and duration depend a great deal on the amount of time the coach has. The weekly conversations cited in the action research project in chapter 4, though ideal, might not be realistic; it is important that principals provide feedback on what frequency and duration they need.

Evaluator as Coach

If the person selected to coach principals is also the person who evaluates principals, a new set of concerns arises. Research on the principal-teacher relationship on coaching and evaluation is relevant to the coach-principal relationship. Glickman (1985) found that the same person can both coach and evaluate teachers if three conditions are present: trust, differentiated behaviors, and knowledge of what is happening when.

> Glickman (1985) found that the same person can both coach and evaluate teachers if three conditions are present: trust, differentiated behaviors, and knowledge of what is happening when.

If the person coaching a principal is also the principal's evaluator, trust is an absolute requirement for the relationship to be successful. In addition, the coach should make sure that the coaching behaviors are distinct from those used in evaluation.

One distinction in the behavior of a coach and an evaluator has to do with the way feedback is provided. Feedback is generally given with the intention of improving performance. However, certain types of feedback decrease, rather than increase, the likelihood for professional growth. Ellison and Hayes (2005) specify five categories of feedback, three of which fit into the category of evaluation and two of which are categorized as coaching.

The types of feedback that are part of Cognitive Coaching are data and mediative questions. Data are specific, observable, measurable, and assessable information that allows the recipient to reflect and respond. Because data have no meaning except what we make of them, the recipient is allowed to make meaning and therefore own the feed-

> *The types of feedback that are part of Cognitive Coaching are data and mediative questions.*

back. When the recipient owns the feedback, the chances of it being used in the future are increased. Following are some examples of data and mediative questions:

> You talked for 10 minutes. Then you said to the staff, "Talk at your tables about the impact this decision might have on your team." Then you did not say anything for 5 minutes. How did you decide what directions to give and how long to give them to talk?

> You started the meeting at 8:00. One staff member came in at 8:10. You looked at her and said nothing. What was going on in your head at that time?

The types of feedback that are used in evaluation are judgments, personal observations, and inferences. A positive judgment will make the person feel good momentarily, but it does not support thinking. Also, if a person can give a positive judgment, that's an indication that he or she can also give a negative one. "You did a great job" tells the observer that you might also be willing to say, "You messed up on that." The anticipation of judgment (positive or negative) from another person not only works against the development of self-directedness, it also shuts down thinking.

Likewise, personal observations do not support the thinking of the recipient. If the observer gives personal opinions, advice, and suggestions, then the recipient becomes other-directed, focusing less on effectiveness and more on the thinking and feeling of the observer. When we hear personal observations, such as "It would have been helpful if you had charted the directions," we tend to become defensive rather than pensive. Our natural reaction is to defend why we did it the way we did rather than to think about the positive outcome of the suggestion.

Inferences, the third evaluation category, are statements that contain vague, unclear, or nonspecific language. They require the recipient to read between the lines to figure out the intended meaning of the observer. Instead of supporting thinking, inferences cause the recipient to wonder what is meant by the feedback. The observer often uses vocabulary that he or she thinks has implicit meaning; for the recipient to understand, however, the terminology has to be made explicit. An example of such feedback is when an observer says, "You used different groupings during the meeting." This feedback might cause the recipient to think, "Does that mean different groups of teachers during the meeting, different groups from the last meeting, or different ways to get staff into groups?" Knowing what specific behavior the observer is referring to gives clarity to the meaning of the feedback.

The observer can usually turn inferences into data by thinking, "What causes me to say that?" For example, in the above scenario, the following statement would have-provided data: "You divided the staff into smaller groups at two different times: one time you used learning partners, and one time you asked them to find a partner at another table." This specific data would allow the recipient to reflect on the decision to use small-group interaction and to become conscious of the decision-making criteria. When data are coupled with mediative questions, the coach has the makings of a rich conversation designed to support the thinking and enhanced behavior of the coachee. Research indicates that Cognitive Coaching promotes personal and professional growth in teachers (Edwards, 2005); there is little evidence in the research on evaluation that teachers grow professionally as a result of being evaluated.

Finally, if the same person is both coach and evaluator, it is imperative that principals know when they are being evaluated and when they are being coached. Costa and Garmston (2002) delineate four support functions: Cognitive Coaching, collaborating, consulting, and evaluating. Each support function represents a different way of relating, depending on one's intentions (see chapter 2). It is essential that intentions and behaviors are aligned; otherwise the person receives a mixed message, which can lead to feelings of being manipulated. It should be clear when one is coaching and when one is evaluating, and one's behaviors should communicate that intention to the principal.

If Cognitive Coaching is the default support function, it is easier to determine whether it is necessary to switch to evaluating and what one might need to say as the evaluator. This can be accomplished in the course of one conversation or in separate conversations. If the response of the principal is a highly emotional one, it might not be possible to return to coaching in the same conversation. In the two examples shown in Table 4-2, the conversations each take a different course. In conversation number 1 the coach evaluator is able to step out of Cognitive Coaching into evaluating and then return to Cognitive Coaching. In conversation number 2, the highly emotional response of the principal causes the coach evaluator to end the conversation and reconnect the next day.

In addition to signaling the switch verbally, the coach/evaluator also needs to use a nonverbal signal. Keeping in mind that a nonverbal message is 65%–85% of what we communicate (Burgoon, Buller, & Woodall, 1989), the coach/evaluator must disengage the rapport established during coaching. Shifting one's body slightly, crossing or uncrossing one's legs, or chang-

Table 4-2. Two Ways to Differentiate Coaching and Evaluating

Conversation No. 1	Conversation No. 2
Principal: Did you hear what that student just said to me? Can you believe it?	*Principal*: Did you hear what that student just said to me? Can you believe it?
Coach Evaluator: You're shocked by the student's rudeness!	*Coach Evaluator*: You're shocked by the student's rudeness!
Principal: Yes!	*Principal*: Yes!
Coach Evaluator: How did you decide what to say in response?	*Coach Evaluator*: How did you decide what to say in response?
Principal: I just reacted and told him to shut up—he needs to know that he can't talk like that in our school!	*Principal*: I just reacted and told him to shut up—he needs to know that he can't talk like that in our school!
Coach Evaluator (disengages rapport): That's not an acceptable response from an adult.	*Coach Evaluator (disengages rapport)*: That's not an acceptable response from an adult.
Principal: I know, but I'm so frustrated with the way these kids talk to each other and to the staff.	*Principal*: I don't care what you say—you don't know what it's like. You haven't been in the schools for a long time! The way these kids behave these days is outrageous—it has to be stopped.
Coach Evaluator: Could I offer you some options?	
Principal: Yes, I'd appreciate your help with this.	*Coach-Evaluator*: You're upset by the behavior of students in your school and your frustra-

cont.

Coach Evaluator: Three things you might do are: (1) Take a deep breath before responding and/or count to 10 before responding; (2) knowing that you are likely to encounter this kind of behavior, think of some acceptable responses ahead of time; (3) take the student to the office and discipline him or her there. [*Reengages rapport*] Which of those options might work for you?

Principal: Well, all of them are helpful. I could do the first and the third. I really like the idea of thinking ahead of time about what to say. Would you help me think of some things?

Coach-Evaluator: Sure.

tion is evident. [*Disengages rapport*] However, no matter how frustrated you are, you cannot speak to students like that.

Principal: So you're suggesting that I just let kids get away with this behavior?

Coach Evaluator: No, that's not at all what I'm saying. I want you to take some time to think about what happened here and then we'll talk tomorrow.

ing one's posture can accomplish this. With rapport disengaged, the coach proceeds to offer the evaluative information. In some cases, the information may be so upsetting to the principal (as in conversation no. 2) that the coach chooses to end the conversation and schedule another meeting. In other cases, the coach might be able to reengage rapport and continue coaching (as in conversation no. 1). Regardless of which support function is chosen, it is important to maintain a focus on self-directedness.

> *Regardless of which support function is chosen, it is important to maintain a focus on self-directedness.*

This can be achieved if attention is

given to: (a) how the coach switches support functions, and (b) strategies that support self-directedness. Although evaluation involves providing external feedback, if the coach maintains a focus on providing data and asking mediative questions, the likelihood of promoting self-directedness is greater.

The action research project described in chapter 3 indicated that of the 14 principals and assistant principals responding, 7 thought it was somewhat important and 6 thought it was very important that their Cognitive Coach was not their supervisor. Only 1 responded that it was not at all important that their coach and their evaluator were different people. Some of the comments from the survey were as follows:

> I believe in and practice direct and honest communication with my supervisors; coaching with a third party confidante clarified my thinking beforehand.
> It was nice to be able to not worry about judgments and to be completely honest.

> It helped me feel like I was under no pressure to "say the right thing."

> Even though my trust in my supervisor is complete, I think it is human nature to put your best foot forward.

> A nonsupervisory coach increases feelings of confidentiality, risk taking in revealing inner thoughts, and emotions that lead to deeper thinking.

> The trust relationship was developed very easily with the coach due to the fact that she was an "outside party"—much like a therapist's relationship with a client.

If the district cannot separate the two functions, the coach evaluator has to be sure to have or develop a trusting relationship with the principal and to pay special attention to when one is coaching and when one is evaluating. This requires high consciousness as well as craftsmanship. If the distinction is not acknowledged and maintained, there is little chance the principal will benefit from coaching by an evaluator.

Experience as a Principal

The question of whether or not the coach must have experience as a principal requires more exploration. In the study described in chapter 4, 11 administrators believed that experience as a principal was very important, and 3 believed that it was somewhat important. Given that a Cognitive Coach is a nonjudgmental, neutral person in a coaching conversation, experience as a principal might not be as important as initially perceived. It is true that a person without experience might be less qualified to step out of Cognitive Coaching to consult or collaborate, but a Cognitive Coach without principal experience might have other experience that would be valuable when consulting or collaborating with a principal. In the action research project, some of the topics the coach consulted about did not come from having experience as a principal. They were topics such as paraphrasing, change, transition, and decision making. Leadership experience in a district, not necessarily principal experience, might be valuable in coaching principals.

Contracting With a Coach

Once the decision is made as to who should coach principals, a conversation should be conducted with the coach to establish a contract; if the coach is external to the system, this conversation should also include the specifics of compensation. The contract may be formal or informal; in either case, Garmston and Wellman (1999) indicate that a successful contracting conversation should contain the following elements: relationship, goals, data, and plan.

The element of relationship involves building trust. As indicated earlier, trust might already have been developed; if not, the process begins with the first contact. In addition to building trust, a relationship also includes establishing mutual expectations and clarity about who the client is and what the mutual learning goals are.

Goals involve establishing the desired state or outcome of the coaching. The most effective goals are SMART: specific, measurable, achievable, relevant, and time-bound. If the principal has not requested the coaching (i.e., the coach has been assigned to the principal) the question of who will be involved in defining the indicators of success must be addressed. We recommend that they be focused on the principal's performance and that the coach not share data with the principal's supervisor. This aspect of confidentiality is critical.

Data play an important role in the contracting conversation. Parties should agree on relevant data and who will have responsibility for gathering, monitoring, and reporting data. Analyzing data is a key aspect of Cognitive Coaching, and it is important that the sources of data be reliable and credible. Perceptual data as well as factual data should be considered over the course of a coaching relationship.

A plan should include success indicators; specifics about frequency, duration, and location of the coaching;

> *A plan should include success indicators; specifics about frequency, duration, and location of the coaching; and a procedure for monitoring the process.*

and a procedure for monitoring the process. Shorter sessions are preferable to longer sessions, given the busy schedule of a principal. Recurrent sessions also add to the effectiveness of the process. Coaching sessions at regular intervals make the process ongoing and eliminate the need to take a long time to review and reconnect. Weekly conversations at the beginning of the process are recommended if both parties can determine that frequency to be most desirable.

The person selected to coach a principal should be someone who is trusted, who maintains confidences, and who is trained for the job. Whether the person comes from inside the district or outside will not affect the success of the process to the extent that trust, confidence, and training will. In many cases an internal person may be selected due to budget constraints. All of these decisions should be made thoughtfully and intentionally.

References

Bryk, A., & Schneider, B. (2001). *Trust in schools: A core resource for improvement.* New York: Russell Sage.

Burgoon, J. K., Buller, D. B., & Woodall, W. G. (1989). *Nonverbal communication: The unspoken dialogue.* New York: Harper & Row.

Costa, A., & Garmston, R. (2002). *Cognitive Coaching: A foundation for renaissance schools.* Norwood, MA: Christopher-Gordon.

Edwards, J. (2005). *Cognitive Coaching: A synthesis of the research.* Highlands Ranch, CO: Center for Cognitive Coaching.

Ellison, J., & Hayes, C. (2005). *Cognitive Coaching foundation seminar learning guide.* Norwood, MA: Christopher-Gordon.

Garmston, R., & Wellman, B. (1999). *The adaptive school: A sourcebook for developing collaborative groups.* Norwood, MA: Christopher-Gordon.

Glickman, C. (1985). *Supervision of instruction: A developmental approach.* Boston: Allyn & Bacon.

Tschannen-Moran, M. (2004). *Trust matters.* San Francisco: Jossey-Bass.

Tschannen-Moran, M., & Hoy, W. K. (2000). A multidisciplinary analysis of the nature, meaning and measurement of trust. *Review of Educational Research, 70* (4), 547–593.

5

The Thinking of a Principal's Cognitive Coach

In chapter 4, the skills and experience necessary to coach principals were outlined. This chapter describes the metacognition of a principal's coach; it is the thinking in Cognitive Coaching that distinguishes it from other types of coaching. The focus on self-directed learning requires that the coach think about the neutral and nonjudgmental role in conversations. The Cognitive Coach is unbiased about *what* the person is thinking, but biased that the person *is* thinking.

Identity as a Mediator of Thinking

The metacognition of a Cognitive Coach is based on the coach's identity as a mediator of thinking. Our identity is who we believe we are and is usually held unconsciously. Although it might be unconscious, it is reflected in all our words and actions and is apparent to all those with whom we live and work. Our identity influences our perceptions, interactions, choices, and, ultimately, the way we fulfill our roles and responsibilities in life.

The term *mediator* comes from the work of Reuven Feuerstein (2000) and refers to mediated learning experiences. In a mediated learning experience, a person processes the experience at a deeper level because a mediator is interposed between the event and the learner. Mediated learning experiences lead to deeper, more pervasive change.

Costa and Garmston (2002) explain a mediator in the following way:

> The word *mediate* is derived form the word *middle*. Therefore, mediators interpose themselves between a person and some event, problem, conflict, challenge, or other perplexing situation. The mediator intervenes in such a way as to enhance another person's self-directed learning. (p. 56)

A person whose identity is that of a mediator of thinking believes that one can be neutral and nonjudgmental in supporting another person's thinking toward being self-directed. A mediator of thinking does not solve other people's problems for them, because that would be robbing them of an opportunity to grow. Metaphorically, a mediator shines a spotlight of awareness on another person's thinking. A mediator of thinking ultimately believes in the human capacity for continual growth—in oneself, in others, and in one's capacity to empower others.

It is as a mediator of thinking that each of us holds the greatest potential for supporting the growth and development of another person. When a coach mediates a principal's thinking, the principal's learning is enhanced and there is an increased likelihood of change. From these mediated learning experiences, a principal is able to more fully develop the potential for success as a leader.

Metaphorical Orientations

Costa and Garmston (2002) contrast four metaphorical orientations that people sometimes take when they are not being a mediator of thinking: parent, expert, friend, and boss. These metaphors help us to understand the presuppositions and goals we have when we are not engaging neutrally, without judgment. For many coaches it is the orientation of expert that is problematic to developing one's identity and capacity as a mediator of thinking. Past experience and positive reinforcement for offering advice and suggestions often interferes with becoming a mediator of thinking. In fact, the job title *consultant* communicates to others that you are an expert, someone to be consulted on designated topics.

People who have an expert orientation place high value on their ability to help others by sharing their expertise. Their sense of self-worth is based on how much they know and how much they can share that knowledge and skill with others. They are often promoted and sought out in an organization as a person to go to to have things "fixed." Letting go of an expert orientation as a default position must happen before a coach can develop the identity of a mediator of thinking. It doesn't mean that the coach will never share his or her expertise; when the decision is made to share expertise, however, it will be based on the principal's need to receive it and not on the coach's need to share it.

The expert orientation often causes the coach to default to the support function of consulting. A coach who begins a conversation in the consulting function lowers the efficacy of the principal and builds dependency on the coach. Given the amount of time that the principal will spend with a coach versus the amount of time spent alone, the coach who enters a conversation as a consultant is not doing everything possible to build the self-directedness of the principal.

Entering a conversation from a neutral, nonjudgmental perspective enables the coach to determine if coaching is the most appropriate support function by which to foster self-directedness. It also enables the coach to determine what information to offer while collaborating, consulting, or evaluating. When one's identify is that of a mediator of thinking, one defaults to the support function of coaching, just as a computer defaults to a certain font. It is from this neutral perspective that one can make decisions about what other ways to support the principal.

Support Functions

Chapter 4 highlighted the support functions of Cognitive Coaching and evaluating. If the principal's coach is also responsible for evaluation, there are important elements to be considered in order to maintain an effective relationship. The support function of evaluating brings with it formality and higher stakes.

The support functions of collaborating and consulting are more likely to be chosen by the principal's coach as alternative types of support that are less formal than evaluating. When switching support functions, the coach must always think about maintaining a focus on self-directedness.

Given that the root of the word *collaborating* is "co-labor," this support function is chosen when the coach sees that co-brainstorming or co-planning might be more appropriate than coaching. In collaboration, it is important that the coach pay attention to the principal to ensure that the two of them are contributing equally to the conversation. The coach might need to use the tools of pausing, paraphrasing, probing, and inquiring to draw out the thinking of the principal. As delineated in chapter 4, the coach will need to signal the switch both verbally and nonverbally and use strategies that support self-directedness, even when not coaching. Lipton and Wellman (2002) suggest brainstorming and co-planning as two strategies that can be used in the course of a conversation. In both situations, the intention is to return to coaching after collaborating, in order to build the ownership of the principal. Table 5-1 shows a conversation in which the coach switched from coaching to collaborating and then back to coaching. The second column provides the reader with access to the coach's thinking.

Table 5-1. Combined Coaching and Collaborating

Dialogue	Coach's Thinking
P: Thanks for meeting with me today. I want to go over the agenda for my next staff meeting to see what you think.	
C: So you've planned a staff meeting and you want to review it before finalizing it.	*She wants my feedback on the staff meeting agenda. I paraphrase to be sure that is her intention.*
P: Yes.	
C: OK, why don't you take me through it.	*That is her intention. I want to find out her thinking first, so I ask her to go through the agenda. I will listen for States of Mind in her planning.*
P: Well, I'm starting with a celebration of our moving from a high rating to an excellent rating as a school. Everyone has worked really hard, and I want to acknowledge that. Next we're going to talk about how we can continue to sustain the growth we've achieved, but I'm afraid they're going to think that I think what they've done is not good enough. I'm not sure how to make them feel good about the work they've done and at the same time continue to do even better work.	

cont.

C: (pauses to think before speaking)	*She's conscious of the importance of celebrating the recent success and knows this will build efficacy with the staff. She's struggling with how to maintain their efficacy and at the same time increase their craftsmanship and interdependence. Her consciousness is high.*
C: So on the one hand you want to acknowledge their hard work, and on the other hand you want them to draw on their craftsmanship and interdependence to continue to do well.	*I summarize and paraphrase to let her know that I understand the struggle she's having. She knows Cognitive Coaching, so I use States of Mind terminology.*
P: Yes, that's it.	
C: So when you think about other times when you have supported them in improving, what are some of the ways you've done that?	*She signed off on that paraphrase, so I draw on her efficacy and consciousness by asking how she has done this in the past.*
P: Well, in the past, they've known that what we were doing wasn't good enough, so they wanted to improve. Now I'm afraid that some of them don't see the need to continue the improvement we've started.	

cont.

C: So this is new for you and your staff?	*She has not had this combination of circumstances in the past. I paraphrase to let her know I understand that this is different from other situations that she has dealt with.*
P: Yes!	
C: What might be some of your thoughts about how to do this?	*She agrees, so I inquire about her current thinking to determine how resourceful she is feeling.*
P: Right now, I have none. What do you think?	
C: Well, how about if the two of us brainstorm some ideas?	*She's not feeling at all resourceful about this. She usually has lots of ideas, so perhaps collaborating with her will build her resources. I ask if she would like to collaborate to see if she is in agreement.*
P: That would be great!	
C: (*thinking*)	*She wants to collaborate. So I disengage the rapport we've had in coaching and align myself beside her so we can both work on the agenda. After we brainstorm I will return to coaching by asking, "Which of these do you think might work best for you?"*

Strategies for Supporting Self-Directedness

When a person switches from Cognitive Coaching to consulting, it is especially important that the consulting strategies support self-directedness. The coach looks and listens for indicators that the principal needs another form of support. Consulting strategies should be chosen to fit the content. Each of the strategies is designed to enable the coach to return to the support function of Cognitive Coaching. Lipton and Wellman (2002) suggest four strategies that can be used in the course of a conversation.

Offer a menu

Produce an idea bank

Reference current research

Think aloud

Offering a menu involves naming three or four choices, based on the coach's expertise, from which the principal can choose. Three or four provide options without overwhelming the principal. None of the choices should be given more weight than the others. The intention is to give the principal some ideas, not to encourage doing something in a specific way. The coach can use this strategy by saying, "Could I offer you some options?" or "Would you like to hear some options?" At the end of the consulting, the coach would return to Cognitive Coaching by saying, "Which of those do you think might work for you?" Sometimes the principal says, "Well I don't think any of them are a fit for me, but it makes me think about . . ." In either event, the principal now has greater resourcefulness.

Producing an idea bank follows the same pattern as offering a menu, except that the coach prepares it ahead of time. A menu of options requires the coach to spontaneously have the knowledge and skill the principal needs;

an idea bank allows the coach to plan ahead by anticipating the needs of the principal and preparing. An idea bank can be introduced in the same way as a menu of options. In addition, the coach might consider presenting the ideas in written form and leaving them with the principal.

Sometimes the coach has knowledge of research that would be helpful to the principal. By referencing current research to the principal on a topic of concern, the coach can focus the principal's attention on it and plant seeds for further study.

Sometimes the coach's expertise lies not in options or research, but in the way she thinks about a topic. Sharing this thinking out loud, as a stream of consciousness from the coach's head, allows the principal access to the thinking of an expert and also indicates that even experienced professionals continue to struggle with the complexities of decision-making.

A fifth strategy that can be used in consulting is conducting a role-play. This strategy is useful when the principal is struggling with how to interact with another person or situation. The principal plays the role of the other person, and the coach plays the role of the principal. The coach uses her knowledge and skill to interact in a way that models for the principal how he might interact. To enter the role-play the coach might say, "How about if we role-play this situation? You be the teacher, and I'll be you." After the role-play, the coach might say, "How did that sound (or feel) to you?" The principal can then select the aspects of the role-play that might work for him.

Table 5-2 depicts a conversation in which the coach switched from Cognitive Coaching to consulting by using one of the strategies.

Table 5-2. Combined Coaching and Consulting

Dialogue	Coach's Thinking
P: I'm stuck. I've done everything I know to do, and the staff still expects me to act like their last principal. They loved him, but from what I can tell, he was a patriarch. He solved their problems for them, told them how to do things, and then praised them for doing what he suggested. They want me to do the same thing.	
C: You're frustrated because who you are as a leader is not who your staff wants you to be.	*I pace to let her know I understand the existing state. I label her emotion as frustration and her content as the difference in her leadership style and the expectations of her staff.*
P: Yes! And I can't be who they want me to be. It's not good for them or me.	
C: You're confident in your leadership style and want to be the leader of a self-directed staff.	*She signed off on the paraphrase of her existing state. She is conscious that telling others what to do does not build self-directedness and believes that her leadership style is more effective. I do a shift conceptual focus paraphrase of her goal, characterizing her identity as a leader of a self-directed staff. I want to be sure the goal is broad, a destination, and first party.*

cont.

P: Right! I want them to make decisions and solve problems on their own, but all they want me to do is tell them what they should do.	
C: What do you know about change and transition?	*She is describing the kind of qualities she wants in her staff. She is clear about her goal, but I'm not sure she knows how to help the staff make the transition from their previous principal's style to her style. I ask her what she knows about change and transition to see how much knowledge she has on the topic.*
P: Well, not much. I know that it takes time, but I've given them half a year.	
C: Could I share some thinking about transitions?	*She's not familiar with William Bridge's work. I think if she knew about the phases of a transition, it might help her know how to respond to her staff. I ask permission to switch to consulting and then disengage the rapport we've had to signal nonverbally that I am switching support functions.*
P: Sure.	
C: William Bridges' work suggests that change and transition are not the same things. Change is an event, such as you becoming the principal, and transition is the psychological reorientation to the change.	

cont.

Each of your staff members is experiencing a different psychological reorientation to you. Although the transition is different for each person, it has three phases that are the same for each person: an ending, a neutral zone, and a beginning. Bridges says that we are notoriously bad at making endings and that we hate the chaos of the neutral zone, but that we have to go through those two phases before reaching the new beginning. How might this work connect to what you are experiencing?	*I use a think-aloud strategy to give her Bridges' work in a nutshell and want to see what is connecting for her, so I inquire about her thinking regarding what I've said.*
P: They're in the neutral zone and haven't made an ending—or I haven't made an ending for them, I'm not sure which. So what I'm experiencing with my staff is normal. I'm not doing anything wrong, and neither are they.	
C: So you're clearer about why things are the way they are with your staff.	*She's making connections with her situation. I paraphrase to let her know I understand her new thinking.*
P: Yeah. I don't feel so bad about having done something wrong. It's actually something I haven't done, and now I know where to begin. Could we talk more about how I might create an ending and also deal with the neutral zone?	

cont.

C: Sure. So you want to begin planning for the phases of transition. When would be a good time for us to meet?	*Her efficacy and consciousness are higher. She's no longer blaming herself and is ready to let go of the frustration and plan her next steps. I paraphrase to be sure I understand what she wants to do next and ask when would be a good time for our next meeting.*

The coach used indicators from the principal that a different support function was needed. Take a moment and review these conversations. What were the indicators in each?

Capabilities of a Cognitive Coach

To be a mediator of thinking, one must develop certain capabilities. Garmston and Wellman (1999) explain the meaning of *capability* by contrasting it with *capacity*:

> A capability names what a person is able to do. It is different from a capacity, which refers to how much one can hold. Capabilities are the metacognitive awarenesses with which people determine when to use, how to use, or not to use certain skills. Capabilities therefore organize and direct the use of skills; they influence the application and effectiveness of knowledge and skills. (pp. 33–34)

Costa and Garmston (2002) name four capabilities as metacognitive attributes of a mediator. The capabilities serve as organizing principles that help a coach to know how to behave. Focusing on these capabilities provides the coach with guidance and direction for his or her actions.

Know One's Intentions and Choose Congruent Behavior

Above all else, coaches must be aware of their intentions and make sure that their behavior is congruent with that intention. If the intention is not to coach the principal, that is fine as long as coaching behaviors are not used. A principal will feel manipulated if the coach uses coaching behaviors but really wants the principal to do something a certain way. If the coach wants to influence the principal to do something a certain way, or has information to provide, the coach should be straightforward about these intentions and not try to coach the principal into doing something that the coach wants.

Set Aside Unproductive Patterns of Listening, Responding, and Inquiring

As human beings, we have natural tendencies in the way we listen. As a person is talking, it often triggers our own similar story, causes us to be curious, or elicits us to generate a solution to the situation. These unproductive patterns of autobiographical, inquisitive, and solution listening cause the coach to take the spotlight of awareness off the principal and focus it on the coach. When that happens, the coach is no longer supporting the thinking of the principal. The tools of pausing, paraphrasing, probing, and inquiring are the productive patterns used by a coach who listens. The coach must be aware of when the unproductive patterns are taking over in order to set them aside and stay focused on the principal's thinking.

Adjust One's Style Preferences

Each of us has aspects to our style of interacting that distinguish us from others. Coaches should adjust their style preferences to meet the needs of the principal. Coaches choose to either match or mismatch styles, depending on their intentions. To establish rapport, coaches match styles with the principal. Once rapport is established, coaches may choose to intentionally mismatch styles in order to stretch the principal's thinking. For example, a coach might initially match the big-picture thinking of a principal in a conversation to establish rapport. As the conversation progresses, however, the coach might intentionally ask a question like "What might be the most important thing for you to do about this on Monday morning?" This stretches the principal's thinking by mismatching style with a detailed, rather than a big-picture question.

Navigate Among and Within Support Functions and Maps to Guide Mediational Interactions

Once coaches are skilled with the three conversation maps and the four support functions, they choose the most appropriate map and support function with which to enter each conversation. Once the conversation has begun, the coach continues to navigate by making decisions about when to stay with a support function or map and when to switch.

Table 5-3 summarizes key coaching actions for each capability.

Table 5-3. Coaching Actions for the Four Capabilities

Capability	Coaching Actions
Know one's intentions and choose congruent behavior	• Respond to verbal and nonverbal cues of the principal • Establish rapport • Pause, paraphrase, probe, inquire, pace, and lead with craftsmanship • Signal verbally and nonverbally when switching support functions
Set aside unproductive patterns of listening, responding, and inquiring	• Stay focused on the principal's thinking by setting aside autobiographical, inquisitive, and solution listening • Pause, paraphrase, probe, inquire, pace, and lead with craftsmanship

cont.

Adjust one's style preferences	• Respond to elements of representation system, cognitive style, and educational beliefs in the principal's language. • Match style to establish rapport • Mismatch style to stretch thinking
Navigate among and within support functions and maps to guide mediational interactions	• Default to Cognitive Coaching support function • Skillfully switch support functions • Use the conversation map appropriate to the topic of the conversation • Promote self-directedness, regardless of support function • Engage in formal and informal coaching conversations

Each of the capabilities provides an organizer for parts of the Cognitive Coaching Model. The behaviors of a coach can be categorized by the four capabilities. By focusing on these capabilities a coach actually attends to many coaching behaviors.

A Coach's Metacognition

To more closely examine metacognition in Cognitive Coaching, let's revisit three coaching conversations presented in chapter 2. Two are short and spontaneous; the third is a longer, scheduled meeting. A column has been added to give the reader an example of what might be going on in the mind of a coach during the conversation. After reading each conversation, you might want to make some notes about how your thinking compared to the column describing the coach's thinking.

The conversation in Table 5-4 might take place in a hallway as the principal is walking from one location in the building to another, perhaps on the way to a classroom observation.

Table 5-4. Conversation 1

Dialogue	Coach's Thinking
P: I can't talk long because I have an important meeting to go to with a parent. It's not going to be an easy one.	
C: You're worried about this meeting being especially challenging.	*Although she's really busy she needs a few minutes to talk about an upcoming meeting that she's anticipating will be difficult. I paraphrase to let her know I understand her concern.*
P: Yes, it will be.	
C: What are your goals for the meeting?	*I begin with the Planning Conversation Map, asking her to clarify her goals. She knows there is something beneath the criticism and she wants to find out what it is.*
P: I want to find out what the parents' real concerns are. We seem to get frequent criticism, but I don't know what the real issues are.	
C: So you want to clarify the focus of their anxiety.	*I paraphrase her positive intentions. She "signs off" on the paraphrase.*
P: Yes.	

cont.

C: What would you like to leave the meeting with?	*I probe to help her specify success indicators so she will be clear about how she will know she has gotten to the bottom of their concerns.*
P: That's a helpful question. I think I want to have a specific list of concerns that we can begin to tackle, one by one.	
C: So you have a target now. As you leave, what are you thinking about as actions you will take in the meeting to be certain you leave with the list?	*Her thinking is becoming clearer as she specifies what tangible evidence she will have at the end of the meeting. I paraphrase to let her know I understand her goal and also to watch her to be sure she signs off on the paraphrase. Her head nod tells me that the goal I paraphrased is her goal. Now that she is clear about her outcome and evidence of success, I move to the strategies region of the Planning Conversation Map. Since her time is limited, I begin the strategies region of the map with a walk-away question to engage her consciousness and flexibility. Even though we didn't complete all the regions of the Planning Conversation Map, she has a good start on a plan. I will make a point of asking her later how it went, in order to engage in a reflecting conversation that will support her learning from this experience.*
P: I'll be thinking about that as I go to the meeting.	

Take a moment and review the conversation. How might you compare the coach's thinking to your thinking?

Table 5-5's conversation is also a short, informal one. The principal does not have much time, but the coach wants to use the time they do have to build self-directedness.

Table 5-5. Conversation 2

Dialogue	Coach's Thinking
P: I'd like to talk with you about the staff meeting next week, when we will be doing some analysis of the recent results of our state tests.	
C: You'd like to think through the best way to support teachers in using this new information.	*He's opening the door to a planning conversation. I paraphrase to summarize and organize his thinking and to let him know I understand his outcome.*
P: That would be helpful.	
C: What are some things you hope to accomplish in this meeting?	*His verbal response tells me that he is clear about his goal. I probe to help him be more specific about what he means by "doing some analysis."*
P: Well, I want a celebration of our gains, but simultaneously some acceptance of some of the less positive results.	

cont.

C: So you hope to develop some ownership of the results, both positive and negative.	*He's aware of the importance of celebrating success to build efficacy, and at the same time he wants their consciousness and craftsmanship to be high. I paraphrase using the concept label "ownership."*
P: Yes, and I want a balance of the two.	
C: What would you expect to hear in the meeting or observe that would tell you teachers are feeling ownership of student learning results?	*He signed off on that paraphrase, so now I probe to help identify success indicators.*
P: That's exactly my struggle. Every time we talk about test scores, I get a launching of emotions and a big whine about how unfair it is to do this to us. I am exhausted by it and so tired of the repeated pattern; I just can't seem to stop the spin.	
C: You're tired of the same old behaviors and very uncertain about how to break the pattern in your staff.	*He's struggling with how to get the staff where he wants them. His past experiences have caused high emotion, and he wants to move beyond the emotion to action. He is not resourceful enough to have a Planning Conversation, so I am going to pace him and begin a Problem-Resolving Conversation. I want*

cont.

	to honor the existing state, so I paraphrase his emotion as "tired" and "uncertain" and summarize and organize his content as "how to break the pattern."
P: That's so true. It seems so dramatic. I just wish I could move this forward instead of constantly revisiting the same old issues.	
C: What you want is to be a leader of renewed energy and vision around student learning.	*He signed off on the existing state and is now ready for a goal. His goal has to do with the kind of leader he wants to be. I need to paraphrase it as broad. I frame the goal as his identity as a leader of the kind of staff he wants.*
P: Exactly!	
C: I'm going to leave you with a question that I don't want you to answer now. Just think about it and we'll talk again. What might be some indicators of a staff with renewed energy?	*His verbal and nonverbal behaviors tell me that this is his goal. This is all the time we have, so I will ask a walk-away question that will allow him to continue thinking. I'll check back with him later to see where he is in his thinking.*

Take a moment and review the conversation. How might you compare the coach's thinking to your thinking?

In Table 5-6's conversation, the principal begins what sounds like a Planning Conversation. As the conversation progresses, it becomes a Problem-Resolving Conversation.

Table 5-6. Conversation 3

Dialogue	Coach's Thinking
C: I'm looking forward to working with you this year. How are things going so far?	*I want to let him know that I am glad to be working with him this year and want to see how things are going, so I begin with a question that addresses the first region of the Reflecting Conversation Map.*
P: Being new to this school, I'm working hard to listen, and I'm finding the school to be so very different from my last experience.	
C: You're noticing some things you didn't anticipate.	*I paraphrase to acknowledge what he has said.*
P: That's true.	
C: What are some of the differences you are observing?	*His verbal response tells me that my paraphrase captured what he is thinking. I probe for specificity regarding what he means by "very different." It is important that he is clear about his own thinking.*
P: There seems to be some hesitation to work in teams. I even heard one teacher say that she didn't like to share her ideas with others because the kids would not find them new and fresh when she used them.	

cont.

C: You've discovered that collaboration is not a norm here, and there is even some resistance to the concept of teachers sharing best practices.	*He's concerned and somewhat surprised that teachers do not see collaboration as an effective way to work. I paraphrase with the concept labels "norm," "resistance," and "best practices."*
P: Yes, and it concerns me because we have so many new teachers in the building who need to learn from the veterans.	
C: It's important to you that teachers support one another and learn from one another.	*He values collaboration and sees that both veteran and novice teachers can work together. I paraphrase to shift his focus to values, and he confirms it.*
P: Very much so.	
C: As you analyze the situation, what do you think is the source of the reluctance to share?	*I probe to see what his thinking is as to why teachers are reluctant to collaborate.*
P: I've interviewed several members of the staff and need to interview more. I don't have enough information yet to make a judgment, but it seems to be an issue of trust. I don't see much team planning going on, and some teachers seem very isolated. Some of the staff have told me that there are some members who intimidate others.	

cont.

C: So you've gathered some data from the staff, but you're not sure you have adequate facts to make conclusions yet.	*He has collected data by talking with some staff members individually and plans to talk with others. He is in the process of gathering data and has an idea of the cause, but he would like more information. I paraphrase to acknowledge what he has said and inquire about patterns that are emerging. This will begin the process of analyzing some of the data he has received.*
P: I need to hear from others still.	
C: Based on the information you have, what are some patterns you are beginning to see?	*I inquire as to what meaning he is making of the data by asking about patterns.*
P: Well, there seem to be haves and have-nots. I hadn't thought of it before, but even the most positive folks I've spoken with seem to think the last principal depended on a few folks and they got all the rewards.	
C: So a concern about fair treatment is emerging.	*He's seeing a pattern that is connected to his predecessor. He's gaining insights and making connections to teacher behaviors. I paraphrase using the concept label "fair treatment."*
P: I think that's quite true.	

cont.

C: What other data might you need to collect to test your hypothesis?	*He accepts that label. I inquire to expand his thinking about how he might get more information before reaching a conclusion.*
P: *Fairness* is the right word. That seems to capture it. I know that sometimes one small issue can take on a life of its own, such as one teacher going to a conference and others not having the opportunity. It would be useful to collect some history of how decisions about those kinds of rewards are made. I might be able to create some structures that are different and encourage sharing of learning.	
C: You're thinking that decision making is a key issue in how people perceive fair treatment. You have some ideas about how you might tackle that issue in a way that could also encourage teachers to share.	*The word "fairness" makes sense to him. He's thinking about examples, which causes him to consider decision-making practices and how he might structure things differently. I paraphrase the essence of what he is saying about decision making and fairness and summarize his thinking about ideas to encourage more sharing.*

cont.

P: Yes, I'm comfortable with expecting teachers to share as a contingency for having access to professional development opportunities. I think there are other issues here, but this may be a place to explore the school's climate.	
C: You're starting to frame these issues as school culture.	*He's making a connection between teachers sharing and professional development opportunities, and seeing this as a good starting point for building a more positive school climate. I paraphrase using the broad term "school culture." He's considering the label.*
P: Well, maybe that is the issue.	
C: What are some things you learned in your last school about developing culture?	*To draw on efficacy and consciousness, I inquire about what he has learned in the past about school culture. I want to know how knowledgeable he is about this topic.*
P: My last school had a really strong collaborative culture when I came in as principal, and I didn't have to do much, other than reinforce it and sustain the structures that were in place.	

cont.

C: You're learning that you may need to be a different kind of leader in this school and that a focus for you will be developing a stronger culture.	*He hasn't had experience building a collaborative culture, since he inherited one at his last school. I paraphrase to acknowledge that he is experiencing something different from his previous school, which requires a different type of leadership.*
P: I'm beginning to see things in a new light.	
C: Where does that take you in your next steps in entering this school?	*I probe for specificity about what he's thinking his next steps might be.*
P: That's a challenging question for me. I'm not sure I know how to do that, given my last experience. I think that is an area where I may need to do some studying. One thing that comes to mind is that I need to think about what I am modeling in each interaction that sends a message about what I expect as a leader of a different culture.	
C: Today you are aware that you are going to have to reflect on what you might do to become a different kind of leader. You're clear that the modeling you do on a daily basis will be critical.	*He sees building a collaborative culture as a challenge that he might need support with. He is clear that the behaviors he models will speak volumes to his staff about the culture he envisions. He needs more time to think about this issue. I paraphrase to acknowledge his newfound awareness and his need for more reflecting before taking action.*

cont.

P: Yes, that is a place to start.	
C: How has our time together supported your thinking about how you want to enter this school?	*He sees more reflecting and consciousness about modeling as a good beginning toward building a collaborative culture. I ask a question to cause him to reflect on the coaching process so he can be clear about where he is compared to where he was when we started the conversation.*
P: Hearing myself talk about what I have been thinking has solidified what was in my gut and swirling in my head. I think I know more about some things I need to pay more attention to, and I know I need to reflect more on what leadership might look like in this school. I'm not sure I'm ready to formulate any plans, but I know I need to explore the concept of building school culture. I'm grateful for your help in widening my understanding of what I need to pay attention to.	

cont.

P: Thank you, I'm glad our time has been useful. You're starting to think about who you need to be at this school, in contrast to your last school. We can certainly continue this conversation with that in mind. Let's talk about when we can get together again.	*He's echoing what the research says about teachers talking out loud about their practice. His efficacy, consciousness, and craftsmanship are higher. I extend my appreciation for his willingness to think out loud and acknowledge that the conversation has been useful to him. I do a walk-away paraphrase to indicate my willingness to continue the conversation when he is ready. I suggest scheduling a next time to be sure we meet again in the near future.*

Take a moment and review the conversation. How might you compare the coach's thinking to your thinking?

This chapter has given the reader access to what goes on inside the head of a Cognitive Coach. One of the propositions of Cognitive Coaching is that all behavior is produced by thought and perception. It is the thought and perception of the coach that drives his or her behavior. The coach's metacognition determines if the conversation results in the self-directedness or the other-directedness (i.e., dependency) of the principal. The coach's identity as a mediator of thinking ensures that each conversation begins from a neutral, nonjudgmental perspective. A mediator is intensely curious about what's going on for the principal and tries to always begin a conversation focusing on the principal's thinking. In so do-

> *The coach's metacognition determines if the conversation results in the self-directedness or the other-directedness (i.e., dependency) of the principal.*

ing, the coach can make decisions about how to continue the conversation to best support the self-directedness of the principal. The coach continually assesses States of Mind in order to draw upon the internal resources of the principal. Finally, the coach views the coaching relationship as reciprocal, and continues to learn from each and every conversation.

References

Bridges, W. (1991). *Making the most of change*. Reading, MA: Perseus Books.

Costa, A., & Garmston, R. (2002). *Cognitive Coaching: A foundation for renaissance schools*. Norwood, MA: Christopher-Gordon.

Feuerstein, R. (2000). Mediated learning experience. In A. Costa (Ed.), *Teaching for intelligence II: A collection of articles* (p. 275). Arlington Heights, IL: Skylights.

Garmston, R., & Wellman, B. (1999). *The adaptive school: A sourcebook for developing groups*. Norwood, MA: Christopher-Gordon.

Lipton, L., & Wellman, B. (2002). *Mentoring matters*. Sherman, CT: MiraVia.

6

Options and Structures
for Providing Cognitive
Coaching to Principals

Each system has a unique set of needs and resources related to providing coaching services to its principals. Some organizations have a large number of principals, whereas others have only a few. Some choose to focus coaching efforts on new principals, whereas others choose to support each and every principal through coaching. Some have limited personnel to serve as coaches, whereas others have a plentiful pool of candidates. This chapter explores a menu of options for delivery in order to assist districts in considering what structures might work best in supporting principals.

It is our strong belief that every principal, at every point in his or her career, deserves and can benefit from an ongoing coaching relationship. Professional development has its greatest benefits when it is job embedded. It is not something principals need only in the early years of their careers. Today's principalship is complex, ever changing, and de-

> It is our strong belief that every principal, at every point in his or her career, deserves and can benefit from an ongoing coaching relationship.

manding. Can you imagine a baseball player who did not attend spring training every year? Even experienced principals tell us that having a person to think with enhances their capacity to serve in a thoughtful and professional manner.

One district found that almost 20 principals could be coached for less than the cost of a first-year teacher. By thinking creatively and carefully examining resource use, school districts have found ways to support the coaching of principals. Resources are often utilized in traditional ways. Line items in the budget are rolled over, year after year, without examination of impact. When systems think differently, new visions emerge. What if money spent sending principals to conferences was invested in coaching? What if dollars allocated to principals for discretionary use in professional development were targeted for coaching? What if systems created budget lines for coaching principals as they do for coaching teachers? What if principal institutes were replaced by coaching throughout the year? The possibilities are endless when districts let go of traditional thinking.

We offer you the following grid (Figure 6-1) as a way to think about how a system might look at a structure for providing coaching. It assumes that there are different delivery models to choose from and that organizations will serve their principals by considering which options best serve their needs. One consideration is "Do we use a professional coach detached from the principalship, or should we use peer coaches?" A second choice is "Should we coach in groups or with individuals?"

Individual Coaching by a Professional Coach

Adams 12 Five Star School District in Thornton, Colorado, has made a commitment to support all principals through individual coaching by professionals (quadrant

Figure 6-1. Coaching Structure

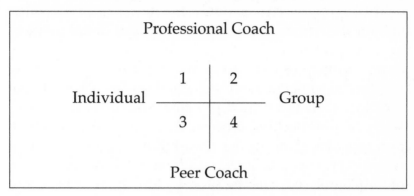

1). Four executive directors have been charged with spending 80% of their time in schools coaching and supporting principals. The process is in its early stages, so data on results still need to be collected. Trust building is an early focus, especially given that coaching of principals is a new role in the system and is unfamiliar to principals. The executive directors are also evaluators of the principals, so there are some fine lines to walk in terms of support functions and trust building. Early implementation is showing that the principals value the coaching. The executive directors discovered early that management issues (e.g., student discipline, budget) still need assistance. By taking the time to work with management issues, the coaches are finding that they can move the principals through daily problems that keep them from being able to address student achievement and instructional concerns. Planning, Reflecting, and Problem-Resolving Conversations characterize the interactions, depending on the needs of the principal. Frequency of visits is becoming important. The executive directors are discovering that the plan to visit schools every 2 weeks might not be frequent enough in early trust-building stages.

Not all systems have the personnel available to provide the kind of coaching to which Adams 12 Five Star has committed. Choices might have to be made as to how to best allocate resources based on defined needs. Many school districts provide coaches only for new principals, often just for their first year. Louisiana has mandated mentors for new principals. We suggest that successful coaching of new principals can best be accomplished by assigning the duty to someone who is charged specifically with that function, such as a retired principal who can focus exclusively on the coaching process. Once again, careful attention must be given to the trust-building process so that the new principal understands the nonjudgmental nature of the Cognitive Coaching process. Ideally, as indicated in chapter 3, the person working with the new principal is not the evaluator.

Another way to think about using limited coaching resources for individual principals is based on school need. Although we believe that all principals should be coached, it is critical that principals in low-performing schools have a system to support them through ongoing improvement processes. In Local District 3 of the Los Angeles Unified School District, coaches work with principals of schools identified as low performing by the state of California. Weekly meetings are scheduled to analyze data, do short- and long-range planning, problem-solve, and focus on improvement goals. The coach provides neutral support to the principal in addition to that provided by a director who is responsible for evaluation of the principal. Schools that have had this level of support are showing performance gains in student achievement. A principal who is coached on a regular basis takes time out of the everyday hubbub to reflect, check on progress, and stay grounded in data. Some of the coaches in Los Angeles have been principals, but most have not. It has been successful to use personnel from the local district office to provide intensive, ongoing support to principals. This is an important finding for districts that may not have a pool of experienced principals on which to draw.

Individual Coaching by Peers

An alternative model to consider is one in which practicing principals coach one another as peers (quadrant 3). If this option is chosen, foundational training in Cognitive Coaching should be provided to all principals. Without training in how to mediate cognition, principals coaching one another can become sessions of sharing "war stories" and giving advice. Principals need to commit to being mediators of one another's thinking if

> *Principals need to commit to being mediators of one another's thinking if genuine capacity is to be built.*

genuine capacity is to be built. Another issue for practicing principals is finding time. We have found that when the coach is also a practicing principal, little coaching of the principal occurs, due to the demands on the time of both principals. If systems are to adopt a peer coaching process, careful attention must be given to structuring for frequent and meaningful interactions. We have observed that this works best when there is an expectation that principals visit each other's schools and that they are held accountable for doing so. The organization has to develop a culture that expects all to be learners through collaborative practices. Some districts have found that by replacing unnecessary information-giving meetings with an expectation of coaching others, far more is gained.

Time can be set aside at regular principal meetings for coaching among colleagues. Most principal groups meet on a monthly basis. By taking a half hour of meeting time, pairs can practice their coaching skills and receive meaningful coaching on issues they have brought to the table. The way an organization uses time is one indicator of what a system values. Setting time for coaching on an agenda creates a culture that values and expects thoughtful practice. It also provides a model for principals to use at their schools with their own staff meetings.

Group Coaching

Group coaching (quadrants 2 and 4) is new territory being explored by the Center for Cognitive Coaching. Group coaching is an even more challenging skill than coaching an individual (Ellison & Hayes, 2003). The dynamics of mediating a group's thinking are far more complex than of mediating an individual's thinking. It requires the coach to attend to the needs of the individuals and to the group as an entity in its own right, a classic dilemma in holonomy. In coaching a group, the coach is noticing the States of Mind of each individual, but is also attentive to the States of Mind of the group. For example, in any group you might have individuals who work as highly flexible principals, but the group itself is not flexible in its shared cognition. Whenever a coach is working with a group, interdependence always requires attention. Without interdependence at high levels, a group is not a true group but merely a set of individuals. Group coaching could be by a peer (quadrant 4) or by a professional coach (quadrant 2). We know of principals who work through local chapters of principal centers to bring together principals from different districts. An ongoing group is formed, and they work as peer coaches for the group, taking turns leading the group coaching session. The advantage of working with peers who are from other districts is the opportunity to learn from other systems.

> *Without interdependence at high levels, a group is not a true group but merely a set of individuals.*

In considering group coaching of principals, a system should evaluate what criteria would be useful in forming a group. Size is one criterion. Three to six seems to be workable; any larger than that reduces each individual's time to contribute. Another criterion is membership characteristics. There is value in balancing diversity around gender, age, and ethnicity. There is also value in finding some common ground for selection of group members.

One example might be a group of principals serving a K–12 articulation area serving the same student population. Another might be by levels, such as all middle school principals. A group could also consist of principals with three or fewer years of experience. Group members could be selected by common issues, such as low math scores for girls or ethnic gaps in student achievement.

An administrative team is another natural group to coach. It might consist of principals and assistant principals in a secondary school. Some elementary leadership teams include teacher coaches working at the building. Sometimes coaches are used over a long term with teams, other times they serve a short-term function, such as observing and collecting data on meetings followed by a reflecting conversation. This short-term coaching could also be related to a specific project a team is working to complete.

When we were part of a central office instructional team in Douglas County School District in Castle Rock, Colorado, the team was part of an effort to provide coaching to school leadership teams regarding the school's achievement. Semi-annual Focus on Achievement Meetings were held to assist the school in making meaning of its achievement data. A team of three or four central office administrators would meet with the school's key leaders, including administrators and teaching staff. The purpose of the first meeting was to have a Reflecting Conversation using the data the school had collected on the achievement of its students. At the end of the reflection, a Planning Conversation was held to target new goals for improvement. Later in the year, a second meeting was held to reflect on progress and to problem-solve as necessary. High value was placed on the interest and support of the central office. The structure caused school leaders to think together in a manner that would not have occurred without the time commitment for group coaching on student achievement. Each school conversation was unique and tailored to the specific needs and choices of the school staff.

> *One person with limited time can serve more principals by working with them as a group.*

Even though group coaching has many challenges, the advantages are also compelling. One person with limited time can serve more principals by working with them as a group. The shared thinking of the group can create knowledge for the group, and for each person in the group, that would not be created alone. The coaching of a group also provides a model for principals on how they might coach groups of teachers at their schools.

Planning for Coaching Principals

The following questions can serve as planning questions for a system intent on implementing a program of Cognitive Coaching for principals:

- What outcomes do we want to achieve through coaching? Does the system want greater retention of principals, gains in student achievement, reduced stress for principals, accelerated professional development, or other outcomes?

- How will we measure the outcomes? What data will be collected on the coaching process?

- What are our resources for coaching? What personnel, budget, and time will be required?

- What training will we need to provide?

- Who should be served?

- Who should do the coaching?

- How can we best serve the principals—individual coaching, group coaching, both?

- How might we structure the coaching of principals in order to achieve our outcomes?

- How will we evaluate the effectiveness of the coaching process?

Taking time to plan carefully, using these questions as a guide, will enhance the likelihood of success for any coaching program. Whatever choices an organization makes, principals will surely appreciate and benefit from receiving support. The mediation of thinking is a key feature of effective support. Wheatley (2005, p. 215) reminds us, "Thinking is the place where intelligent action begins." Cognitive Coaching is about thinking. It provides a resource to principals for intelligent action.

References

Ellison, J., & Hayes, C. (2003). *Cognitive Coaching: Weaving threads of learning and change into the culture of an organization* (chapter 9). Norwood, MA: Christopher-Gordon.

Wheatley, M. (2005). *Finding our way: Leadership for an uncertain time.* San Francisco: Berrett-Koehler.

Appendix

Table A-1. Staff Pre- and Post-Assessment Difference

ADM.	Efficacy	Consciousness	Craftsmanship	Flexibility	Interdependence
1	+1	+1.5	+2.5	+3.3	**-1.8**
2	+1	+.3	-1	**-1.7**	+.3
3	+4.3	+4.5	+3.8	+3.5	+.3
4	+2.2	+3.2	+2.2	+3.4	+1.2
5	-1	+3.8	-1	**-2.4**	**-3.2**
6	+1.6	-.3	+2	+2.3	+.6
7	+7.5	+3	+3.2	+2.2	+3.5
8	**-2.6**	**-2.6**	**-3.3**	**-1.3**	**-5.5**
9	+2.3	+4	+4	+3.3	+5
10	+4.6	+4.2	+4.3	+5.8	+3.7
11		Incomplete	Data		
12	+3	+1	+1.5	+2.1	+3.6
13	+.7	+3.7	+3	+1.6	+1.3
14	+2.2	+.8	+.3	**-2.2**	+1.5
15	**-1.3**	**-2.3**	**-.2**	**-1.5**	+1.3
16	**-2**	-1	-1	-1	**-2**

Table A-2. Supervisors' Pre- and Post-Assessment Difference

ADM.	Efficacy	Consciousness	Craftsmanship	Flexibility	Interdependence
1	+2	+6.5	+4.5	+8.5	+1.5
2	+6	+7	+5	+3	+1
3	+7	+6	+7.5	+10.5	+2
4	+1	+2	+1	−1	−3
5	+5	+7	+6	+7	+2
6		Incomplete	Data		
7	+7	+6	+6	+7	+3
8	+1	−1	−2	−1	+2
9	+8	+6	+6	+7	+8
10	+1	+1	+2	+1	+1
11		Incomplete	Data		
12	0	+3	−1	−5	+6
13	+2	−2	−1	−5	+2
14	+5	+10	+2	+7	+4.5
15		Incomplete	Data		
16	+1	+1	+3	+2	+2

Table A-3. Comparisons of Three Sources of Pre- and Post-Assessment Data

Administrator No. 1 (One decrease from staff in interdependence)

	Efficacy	Consciousness	Craftsmanship	Flexibility	Interdependence
Self	+1.5	+4	+1.5	+3	+1
Staff	+1	+1.5	+2.5	+3.3	**−1.8**
Super-visor	+2	+6.5	+4.5	+8.5	+1.5

Administrator No. 2 (Decreases in two States of Mind each from self and staff)

	Efficacy	Consciousness	Craftsmanship	Flexibility	Interdependence
Self	**−1**	**−2**	+2	+1	+2
Staff	+1	+.3	**−1**	**−1.7**	+.3
Super-visor	+6	+7	+5	+3	+1

Administrator No. 3 (One decrease from self in efficacy)

	Efficacy	Consciousness	Craftsmanship	Flexibility	Interdependence
Self	−2	+2	+4	+1	+2
Staff	+4.3	+4.5	+3.8	+3.5	+.3
Super-visor	+7	+6	+7.5	+10.5	+2

Administrator No. 4 (One decrease from supervisor in flexibility)

	Efficacy	Consciousness	Craftsmanship	Flexibility	Interdependence
Self	+5	+10	+1	+7	+2
Staff	+2.2	+3.2	+2.2	+3.4	+1.2
Super-visor	+1	+2	+1	−1	−3

Administrator No. 7 (All increases)

	Efficacy	Consciousness	Craftsmanship	Flexibility	Interdependence
Self		Incomplete	Data		
Staff	+7.5	+3	+3.2	+2.2	+3.5
Super-visor	+7	+6	+7	+7	+3

Administrator No. 8 (Decreases from self, staff, and/or supervisor in all States of Mind)

	Efficacy	Consciousness	Craftsmanship	Flexibility	Interdependence
Self	–1	+1	+1	+2	–2
Staff	–2.6	–2.6	–3.3	–1.3	–5.5
Super-visor	+1	–1	–2	–1	+2

Administrator No. 5 (Decreases from self or staff in all States of Mind except consciousness)

	Efficacy	Consciousness	Craftsmanship	Flexibility	Interdependence
Self	–1	+1	0	–3	–2
Staff	–1	+3.8	–1	–2.4	–3.2
Super-visor	+5	+7	+6	+7	+2

Administrator No. 6 (One decrease from staff in consciousness)

	Efficacy	Consciousness	Craftsmanship	Flexibility	Interdependence
Self	+5.5	+5	+5.5	+4	+3.5
Staff	+1.5	–.3	+2	+2.3	+.6
Super-visor		Incomplete	Data		

Administrator No. 9 (One decrease from self in craftsmanship)

	Efficacy	Consciousness	Craftsmanship	Flexibility	Interdependence
Self	+1	+5	-5	+7	+4
Staff	+2.3	+4	+4	+3.3	+5
Super-visor	+8	+6	+6	+7	+8

Administrator No. 10 (All increases)

	Efficacy	Consciousness	Craftsmanship	Flexibility	Interdependence
Self	+6	+6	+4	+1	+3
Staff	+4.6	+4.2	+4.3	+5.8	+3.7
Super-visor	+1	+1	+2	+1	+1

Administrator No. 11 (All increases with incomplete data)

	Efficacy	Consciousness	Craftsmanship	Flexibility	Interdependence
Self	0	+4.5	+5.5	+3	+5.5
Staff		Incomplete	Data		
Super-visor		Incomplete	Data		

Administrator No. 12 (Decreases in three States of Mind from self or supervisor)

	Efficacy	Consciousness	Craftsmanship	Flexibility	Interdependence
Self	–1	0	+1	+3	+3
Staff	+3	+1	+1.5	+2.1	+3.6
Super-visor	0	+3	–1	–5	+6

Administrator No. 13 (Decreases in three States of Mind from supervisor)

	Efficacy	Consciousness	Craftsmanship	Flexibility	Interdependence
Self	+3	+1	+5	+3	+5
Staff	+.7	+3.7	+3	+1.6	+1.3
Super-visor	+2	–2	–1	–5	+2

Administrator No. 14 (All increases)

	Efficacy	Consciousness	Craftsmanship	Flexibility	Interdependence
Self	+6	+6	+1	+6	+4
Staff	+2.2	+.8	+.3	+2.2	+1.5
Super-visor	+5	+10	+2	+7	+4.5

Administrator No. 15 (Decreases in all States of Mind from self or staff)

	Efficacy	Consciousness	Craftsmanship	Flexibility	Interdependence
Self	+1	+1	+2	0	–1
Staff	–1.3	–2.3	–.2	–1.5	+1.3
Super-visor		Incomplete	Data		

Administrator No. 16 (Decreases in all States of Mind from staff)

	Efficacy	Consciousness	Craftsmanship	Flexibility	Interdependence
Self	+1	+4.5	+2	+1	+3.5
Staff	–2	–1	–1	–1	–2
Super-visor	+1	+1	+3	+2	+2

Table A-4. Administrator "Post-Pre-" and Post-Assessment Difference

	Efficacy	Consciousness	Craftsmanship	Flexibility	Interdependence
1	+4.5	+3	+.5	0	+1
2	0	0	+3	+1.5	+1
3	+2	+3	+5	0	+5
4	+1	+7	+2	+2	−1
5	+4.5	+3	+2	+2	0
6	+6	+6	+8.5	+7	+8.5
7		INCOMPLETE	DATA		
8	0	0	0	+1	+1
9	+2	+1	−1	+4	+1
10	+5	+5	+3	+4	+3
11	+7.5	+7.5	+4	+3.5	+7
12	−2	+1	+3	+2	+5
13	+8	0	+5	+4	+4
14	+5	+5	+1	+5	+2
15	+5	+2	+4	+3	+4
16	0	+1	+2	+2	+3

Index

About the Authors

Jane Ellison, Ed.D., is an independent consultant and Co-Director of two corporations, the Center for Cognitive Coaching and Kaleidoscope Associates. Jane provides consultation to school districts and other organizations in the areas of Cognitive Coaching^SM, Adaptive Schools, change and transition, learning-focused leadership, quality professional development, and facilitation. She is the co-author with Carolee Hayes of *Cognitive Coaching: Weaving Threads of Learning and Change Into the Culture of an Organization.*

Jane was the director of Elementary Education for Douglas County School District R-1 in Castle Rock, Colorado from 1988 to 1998. In that position, Jane was responsible for the development of elementary standards and curriculum, the monitoring of instruction, and the supervision of principals.

Jane was a principal for 15 years—4 in Douglas County, Colorado and 11 in Tinley Park, Illinois. Her teaching experience is in the primary grades and at the graduate college level. She holds a B.A. in Elementary Education and Social Sciences from SMU, an M.Ed. in Elementary Supervision from the University of North Texas, and an Ed.D. in Administration from VPI&SU, Blacksburg, Virginia. She is licensed as a teacher and supervisor in Texas and as an administrator in Colorado.

Jane's experiences include teaching graduate classes in South America, attending the Principals' Institutes at Columbia Teachers' College and Harvard University, and chairing the board of directors of the Principal's Center at the University of Colorado, Denver. She is also a certified teacher and principal perceiver specialist.

Carolee Hayes, M.A., is an independent consultant and co-director of two corporations, the Center for Cognitive Coaching and Kaleidoscope Associates. Carolee provides consultation to school districts and other organizations in the areas of Cognitive Coaching[SM], Adaptive Schools, change and transition, learning-focused leadership, quality professional development, and facilitation. She is the co-author with Jane Ellison of *Cognitive Coaching: Weaving Threads of Learning and Change Into the Culture of an Organization.*

Carolee was the director of staff development for Douglas County School District R-1 in Castle Rock, Colorado from 1989 to 1998. She developed and directed the nationally recognized Building Resource Teacher program that places a staff developer in every school.

Prior to working for Douglas County, Carolee was a staff developer and middle school teacher in Jefferson County School District R-1. She holds a B.A. in Family Studies from Colorado Women's College and an M.A. in Curriculum and Instruction from the University of Denver. She is licensed as a secondary teacher and administrator.

Carolee is a wife, a mother, and the grandmother of three wonderful children who inspire her work to support quality public education.